arc42 by Example

Software architecture documentation in practice

Dr. Gernot Starke

Michael Simons

Stefan Zörner

Ralf D. Müller

arc42 by Example

Authors: Dr. Gernot Starke, Michael Simons, Stefan Zörner, and Ralf D. Müller

Managing Editor: Snehal Tambe

Acquisitions Editor: Bridget Neale

Production Editor: Samita Warang

Editorial Board: Shubhopriya Banerjee, Bharat Botle, Ewan Buckingham, Mahesh Dhyani, Taabish Khan, Manasa Kumar, Alex Mazonowicz, Bridget Neale, Dominic Pereira, Shiny Poojary, Erol Staveley, Ankita Thakur, Nitesh Thakur, and Jonathan Wray

First Published: October 2019

Production Reference: 1041019

ISBN: 978-1-83921-435-6

Published by Packt Publishing Ltd.

Livery Place, 35 Livery Street

Birmingham B3 2PB, UK

Table of Contents

III - Mass Market Customer Relationship Management   43

Acknowledgements

Dr. Gernot Starke

Long ago, on a winter's day in 2004, I sat together with Peter Hruschka, a long-time friend of mine and discussed one of our mutual favorite subjects – the structure and concepts of software systems. We reflected on an issue we had both encountered often within our work, independent of client, domain, or technology: developers know their way around implementation/technologies; managers know their way around budgets and risk management. But when forced to communicate (or even document) the architecture of systems, they often start inventing their own specific ways of articulating structures, designs, concepts, and decisions.

Peter talked about his experience in requirements engineering: he introduced me to a template for requirements, a prestructured cabinet (or document) called VOLERE, which contains placeholders for everything that might be important for a specific requirements document. When working on requirements, engineers, therefore, didn't need to think long before they dumped their results in the right place – and others would be able to retrieve them later on (as long as they knew about VOLERE's structure). This requirements template had been used in the industry for several years – there even was a book available on its usage and underlying methodology.

"If we only had a similar template for software architecture," Peter complained, and continued, "countless IT projects could save big time and money." My developer soul added a silent wish: "If this was great, it could even take the ugliness out of documentation." We both looked at each other, and in that second decided to create exactly that: a template for software architecture documentation (and communication) that was highly practical, allowed for simple and efficient documentation, was usable for all kinds of stakeholders, and could facilitate software architecture documentation. And, of course, it had to be open source – completely free for organizations to use.

That's how the arc42 journey started. Since then, Peter and I have used arc42 in dozens of different IT systems within various domains. It has found significant acceptance within small, medium, and large organizations throughout the world. We have written many articles about it, taught it to more than 1,000 (!) IT professionals, and included it in several of our software architecture-related books. Thanks, Peter for starting this wild ride with me. And, of course, for your lectures on cooking. Thanks to my customers and clients – I have learned an incredible amount from working together with you on your complex, huge, difficult, interesting, and sometimes stressful problems. Due to all those nondisclosure agreements I have signed in my life, I'm not officially allowed to mention you all by name.

Thanks to my wife, Cheffe Uli, and my kids, Lynn and Per, for allowing dad to (once more) sit on the big red chair and ponder another book project... You're the best, and I call myself incredibly lucky to have you! Thanks to my parents, who, back in 1985, when computer stuff was regarded as something somewhere between crime and witchcraft, encouraged me to buy one (an Apple II, by the way) and didn't even object when I wanted to study computer science instead of something (at that time) more serious. You're great!

Michael Simons

I met Dr. Gernot and Peter (Hruschka) as instructors on a training course at the end of 2015. The training course was called "Mastering Software Architectures" and I learned an awful lot from both of them; not only the knowledge they shared, but how they both shared it. By the end of the training, I could call myself a "Certified Professional for Software Architecture," but what I really took home was the wish to structure, document, and communicate my own projects as Peter and Dr. Gernot proposed, and that's why the current documentation of my pet project, *biking2*, was created.

Since then, I have used arc42-based documentation several times: for in-house products and also for projects and consultancy gigs. The best feedback I've had was something along the lines of: "Wow, now we've got an actual idea about what is going on in this module." What helped that special project a lot was the fact that we were fully set on Asciidoctor and the "Code as documentation and documentation as code" approach I described in depth in my blog. So, here's to Dr. Gernot and Peter: thanks for your inspiration and the idea for arc42.

Stefan Zörner

Originally, DokChess was a case study from my German book on documenting software architecture. Dr. Gernot encouraged me to write it after I told him about the chess example at a conference in Munich in 2011. Thank you especially for that, Dr. Gernot (besides many valuable discussions and good times since then in Cologne, Zurich)! Thanks to my Embarc colleague, Harm Gnoyke, for trying to save my miserable English. All mistakes are my fault, of course.

Ralf D. Müller

Quite a while ago, I discovered the arc42 template as an MS Word document. It didn't take long to see how useful it is and I started to use it in my projects. Soon, I discovered that MS Word wasn't the best format for me as a developing architect. I started to experiment with various text-based formats, such as Markdown and AsciiDoc, but also with wikis. The JAX conference was the chance to exchange my ideas with Dr. Gernot. He told me that Jürgen Krey had already created an AsciiDoc version of the arc42 template. We started to consider this template as the golden master (this is now 5 years ago – in 2014) and tried to generate all other formats needed (at that time, mainly MS Word and Confluence) from this template. The arc42-generator was born, and a wonderful journey was about to start. The current peak of this journey is docToolchain – the evolution of arc42-generator. Read more about its architecture in this book.

On this journey, I have met many people who helped me along the way – it's impossible to name all of them. However my biggest "Thanks!" goes out to Dr. Gernot who always encouraged me to take my next step and helped me along the way. Thank you, Peter and Dr. Gernot, for pushing my architectural skills to the next level through your superb training workshops. Thanks to Jakub Jabłoński and Peter for their review of the architecture – you gave great feedback! Last but not least, I have to thank my family for their patience while I spent too much time with my notebook!

All of us

Thanks to our thorough reviewers, who helped us improve the examples – especially Jerry Preissler, Roland Schimmack, and Markus Schmitz.

Disclaimer

We like to add a few words of caution before we dive into arc42 examples:

> **Note**
>
> We show you quite pragmatic approaches to software and system architecture documentation, based upon the (also pragmatic) arc42 template. Although fine for many kinds of systems, this pragmatism is not appropriate for critical or high-risk systems, developed or operated under strict safety-, security- or similar requirements. If you're working on safety-critical or otherwise potentially dangerous systems, the methods or techniques demonstrated in this book might not be appropriate for you. We, the authors, cannot take any responsibility if you decide to use arc42 or any other approach shown in this book.

The content of this book has been created with care and to the best of our knowledge. However, we cannot assume any liability for the up-to-date, completeness, accuracy or suitability to specific situations of any of the pages.

Preface

About

This section briefly introduces the authors and what the book covers.

About the Book

When developers document the architecture of their systems, they often invent their own specific ways of articulating structures, designs, concepts, and decisions. What they need is a template that enables simple and efficient software architecture documentation. *arc42 by Example* shows how this is done through several real-world examples.

Each example in the book, whether it is a chess engine, a huge CRM system, or a cool web system, starts with a brief description of the problem domain and the quality requirements. Then, you'll discover the system context with all the external interfaces. You'll dive into an overview of the solution strategy to implement the building blocks and runtime scenarios. The later chapters also explain various crosscutting concerns and how they affect other aspects of a program.

About the Authors

Dr. Gernot Starke is an INNOQ Fellow and is the cofounder and a longstanding user of the arc42 documentation template. For more than 20 years, he has been working as a software architect, coach, and consultant, conquering the challenges of creating effective software architectures for clients from various industries. Dr. Gernot cofounded the International Software Architecture Qualification Board (iSAQB e.V.) and the open source Architecture Improvement Method. Dr. Gernot has authored several (German) books on software architecture and related topics.

Michael Simons works as a senior software engineer for Neo4j. Previously, he worked at Enerko Informatik, an Aachen-based company dealing with GIS systems. He has a background focused on geographic information systems for utilities and price calculation for the energy market. In his brief time at INNOQ, he helped customers modernize their application systems. Michael is known for having a certain passion for SQL and Spring. He took his apprenticeship at the FZ Jülich and studied at FH Aachen, Campus Jülich. He is a PRINCE2 ® registered practitioner and sometimes gets torn between the roles of an architect and project manager. Michael is a dedicated blogger and is engaged in various open source projects; you'll find his stuff at michael-simons. eu. He is also a father of two, husband, geek, and passionate cyclist.

Stefan Zörner has 20 years of experience in IT and always looks to the future with excitement. He supports clients in solving architecture and implementation problems. In interesting workshops, he demonstrates how to use practical design tools, as well as spreading enthusiasm for real-life architectural work.

Ralf D. Müller is a solutions architect and an ambitious Grails developer. He is continually trying to simplify his work. Currently, his main concern is improving the holistic documentation of projects. He achieves this especially with the help of the arc42 template and docs-as-code approach. He is the founder of the *docToolchain* project.

Learning Objectives

By the end of this book, you will be able to:

- Utilize arc42 to document a system's physical infrastructure

- Learn how to identify a system's scope and boundaries

- Break a system down into building blocks and illustrate the relationships between them

- Discover how to describe the runtime behavior of a system

- Know how to document design decisions and their reasons

- Explore the risks and technical debt of your system

Audience

This book is for software developers and solutions architects who are looking for an easy, open source tool to document their systems. It is a useful reference for those who are already using arc42. If you are new to arc42, this book is a great learning resource. Those of you who want to write better technical documentation will benefit from the general concepts covered in this book.

Approach

This book follows a teach-by-example approach. It clearly explains how to create comprehensive and easy-to-read documentation using the arc42 template. The book uses real-world applications as case studies and demonstrates how to write documentation for them.

Conventions

New terms and important words are shown like this: "In the preceding diagram, the **mandator** represents an arbitrary company or organization serving mass market customers."

Chapter and Section Numbering

We use Roman numeral chapter numbers (I, II, III, and so on), so we have the Arabic numbers within chapters in alignment with the arc42 sections. In the sections within chapters, we add the chapter prefix only for the top-level sections. That leads to the following structure:

Chapter II: HTML Sanity Checking

II.1 Introduction and Goals

II.2 Constraints

II.3 Context

...

Chapter III: Mass Market CRM

III.1 Introduction and Goals

III.2 Constraints

III.3 Context

...

> **Note**
>
> The first example (HTML Sanity Checking) contains short explanations on the arc42 sections, formatted like this one.

In this book, we keep these explanations to a bare minimum, as there are other books that extensively cover the arc42 background and foundations.

1

I - Introduction

This chapter explains the following topics:

- What is arc42?
- Why this book?
- What this book is not!
- An overview of cxamplcs
- A table of arc42 sections

This book contains several examples of *Software Architecture Documentation* based upon the practical, economical, well-established, and systematic arc42 approach.

It shows how you can communicate about software architectures, but it does not show you how to develop or implement systems!

I.1 What is arc42?

arc42 is a template for architecture documentation.

It answers the following two questions in a pragmatic way, but can be tailored to your specific needs:

- *What* should we document/communicate about our architecture?
- *How* should we document/communicate it?

Figure 1.1 gives you the big picture: it shows a (slightly simplified) overview of the structure of arc42:

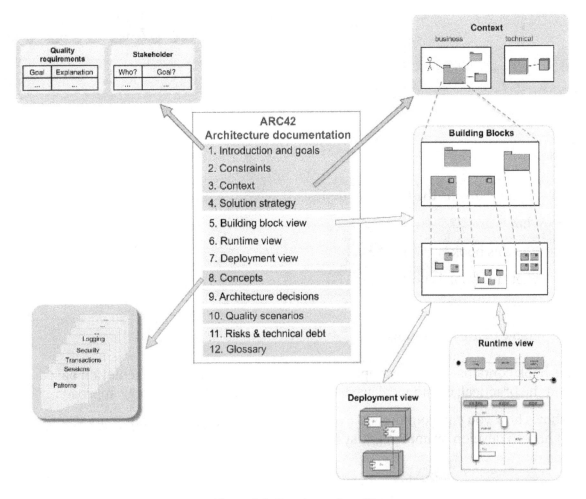

Figure 1.1: Structure of arc42

Compare arc42 to a cabinet with drawers: the drawers are clearly marked with labels indicating the content of each drawer. arc42 contains 12 such drawers (a few more than you see in the diagram that follows). The meaning of these arc42 drawers is easy to understand:

Figure 1.2: arc42 drawers

arc42 offers you a simple and clear structure to document and communicate your (complex!) system. Starting with the goals and requirements of your system and how its embedded into its environment, you can provide the important stakeholders of your system with adequate information about the architecture.

arc42 is optimized for understandability and adequacy. It guides you to explain any kind of architecture information or decision in an understandable and reproducible context.

Individuals and organizations using arc42 especially like two things about it:

1. The understandability of the documentation, resulting from its standardized structure (the drawers)

2. The manageable amount of effort needed to create such documentation - we call it "painless documentation"

Why arc42?

You're kidding, aren't you? Ever heard of Douglas Adams, the (very British) and already deceased sci-fi writer? His novel *Hitchhikers Guide to The Galaxy* calls arc42 the:

Answer to the Ultimate Question of Life, The Universe, and Everything (https:// en.wikipedia.org/wiki/Phrases_from_The_Hitchhiker's_Guide_to_the_ Galaxy#Answer_to_the_Ultimate_Question_of_Life.2C_the_Universe.2C_and_ Everything_.2842.29)

arc42 aims to provide the answer to *everything* related to your software architecture. (Yes, I know it's a little pretentious, but we couldn't think of a better name back in 2005.)

Where to Get Additional Information

With the latest release (V7) of arc42 in January 2017, the project now has extensive online help and FAQs (frequently asked questions) available:

- The documentation site docs.arc42.org (https://docs.arc42.org) contains the full documentation plus many (more than 100) tips for efficient and effective usage.

- The FAQ site faq.arc42.org (https://faq.arc42.org) answers more than 100 typical questions.

I.2 Why This Book?

> **Note**
>
> Examples are often better suited to show how things can work than lengthy explanations.

arc42 users have often asked for examples to complement the (quite extensive) conceptual documentation of the template, which was, unfortunately, only available in German for several years.

There were a few approaches to illustrating how arc42 can be used in real-world applications, but those were (and still are) scattered around numerous sources, and are not carefully curated.

After an incredibly successful (again, German-only) experiment to publish one single example as a (very skinny) 40-page booklet, we decided to publish a collection of examples on a modern publishing platform – so we can quickly react to user feedback and add further samples without any hassle.

I.3 What This Book is Not

In this book, we focus on examples for arc42 to document and communicate software architectures. We only give a brief introduction to arc42 (if you'd like to know more, see *Appendix* B for details).

This book is *not* an introduction to:

- Software architecture

- Architecture and design patterns

- Modeling, especially **UML** (**Unified Modeling Language**)

- Chinese cooking (but you probably didn't expect that here)

I.4 An Overview of Examples

We have encountered exciting software and system architectures during our professional lives. Several of those would have made instructive, interesting, and highly relevant examples – too bad they were declared confidential by their respective owners. Our nondisclosure agreements stated that we're not allowed to even mention clients' names without violating those contracts.

Therefore, it has been quite difficult to find practical examples that we can freely write and talk about.

Now, let's get an overview of the examples that are waiting in the rest of this book.

HTML Sanity Checking

The HTML Sanity Checker is a tiny open source system for checking HTML files for semantic errors such as broken cross-references, missing images, unused images, and similar stuff.

Dr. Gernot wrote the initial version of this system himself when working on a rather large (100+ pages) documentation based upon the AsciiDoctor (https://asciidoctor.org) markup language.

HtmlSanityCheck (or **HtmlSC** for short) is described in *Chapter 2, HTML Sanity Checking*, of this book.

Mass Market Customer Relationship Management

Gosh, what an awkward name – so, let's shorten it to **MaMa-CRM**: mass market refers to consumers of several kinds of enterprises, such as health insurance, mobile telecommunications, or large real-estate companies.

We are reasonably sure you know these 86 × 54 mm plastic cards (experts call them ISO/IEC 7810 – https://en.wikipedia.org/wiki/ISO/IEC_7810). Chances are, you even own several of these cards. If they contain your photo, the chances are high that they were produced by a system such as MaMa-CRM.

MaMa-CRM takes the burden of (usually paper-based) customer contacts from organizations working in such mass markets. It was initially built by an independent mid-sized data center to support the launch of the German (government-enforced) *e-Health Card* and was later used to support campaigns such as telephone billing, electrical-power metering, and similar stuff.

The architecture of MaMa-CRM is covered in *Chapter 3, Mass Market Customer Relationship Management*.

biking2

biking2 or "*Michis mileage*" is a web-based application for tracking biking-related activities. It allows the user to track the mileage covered, collect GPS tracks of routes, convert them to different formats, track the location of the user, and publish pictures of bike tours.

The architecture of **biking2** is covered in *Chapter 4, biking2*.

DokChess – a Chess Engine

DokChess is a fully functional chess engine. The architecture of **DokChess** is covered in *Chapter 5, DokChess*.

docToolchain

docToolchain (https://doctoolchain.github.io/docToolchain) is a heavily used and highly practical implementation of the **docs-as-code** (https://docs-as-co.de) approach. The basic idea is to facilitate the creation and maintenance of technical documentation.

The architecture of **docToolchain** is covered in *Chapter 6, docToolChain*.

MiniMenu

MiniMenu surely has some of the *leanest* architecture documentation you will ever encounter. It captures some design and implementation decisions for a tiny MacOS menu bar application.

The main goal is to show that arc42 even works for very small systems. Skip to *Chapter 7, Mac OS Menubar Application*, to see for yourself.

I.5 A table of arc42 Topics

This table will help you to quickly find the arc42 topics you're looking for. For each section of arc42, you'll find references to each of the book's examples. The digits after the links denote the size of the section in the respective example. We have marked the most extensive or complete examples in bold so that you can easily recognize them:

arc42-Section	Where to Find
1.Introduction and Goals	HtmlSC (5), MaMa-CRM (12), biking2 (2), DokChess (2), docToolchain (5)
2.Constraints	HtmlSC (1), MaMa-CRM (1), biking2 (3), DokChess (2), docToolchain (1)
3.Context	HtmlSC (3), MaMa-CRM (4), biking2 (3), DokChess (2), docToolchain (4)
4.Solution Strategy	HtmlSC (1), MaMa-CRM (1), biking2 (1), DokChess (3),docToolchain (3)
5.Building Block View	HtmlSC (6), MaMa-CRM, biking2 (12), DokChess, docToolchain (2)
6.Runtime View	HtmlSC (2), MaMa-CRM (3), biking2 (2), DokChess (2), docToolchain (0)
7.Deployment View	HtmlSC (3), MaMa-CRM (2), biking2 (1), DokChess (2), docToolchain (4)
8.Crosscutting Concepts	HtmlSC (6), MaMa-CRM (5), biking2 (9), DokChess (7), docToolchain (1)
9.Decisions	HtmlSC (1), MaMa-CRM (1), biking2 (2), DokChess (5), docToolchain (3)
10.Quality Scenarios	HtmlSC (1), MaMa-CRM (2), biking2 (1), DokChess (2), docToolchain (2)
11.Risks and Technical Debt	HtmlSC (1), MaMa-CRM (1), biking2 (1), DokChess (2), docToolchain (2)
12.Glossary	HtmlSC (1), MaMa-CRM (1), biking2 (4), DokChess (3), docToolchain (1)

Figure 1.3: Table of arc42 topics

II - HTML Sanity Checking

By **Dr. Gernot Starke**

The system that's documented in this lesson is a small open source tool that's hosted on GitHub (https://github.com/aim42/htmlSanityCheck).

The full source code is available from the preceding link – you may even want to configure your Gradle build to use this software. If you're writing documentation based on **Asciidoctor**, this would be a great idea!

But enough preamble. Let's get started.

II.1 Introduction and Goals

This section will explain the driving forces for architecturally relevant decisions and important use cases or features, all of which will be summarized in a few sentences. If possible, refer to the existing requirements documentation.

The main goal of this section is to ensure that your stakeholders understand the solution at hand.

`HtmlSanityCheck` (`HtmlSC`) supports authors creating digital formats by checking hyperlinks, images, and similar resources.

1.1 Requirements Overview

> **Note**
>
> If you would like to have a brief explanation of the important goals and requirements, use cases, and features of the system, please refer to the existing requirements documentation.
>
> It's important that you understand the central tasks of the system before you take a look at the architecture of the system (starting with arc42-section 3).

The overall goal of HtmlSC is to create neat and clear reports that show errors within HTML files. The following is a sample report:

Figure 2.1: Sample report

HtmlSanityCheck (**HtmlSC**) checks HTML for semantic errors such as broken links and missing images. It was created to support authors who create HTML as an output format. This operation can be explained as follows:

1. Authors write in formats such as AsciiDoc (https://asciidoctor.org/docs/what-is-asciidoc/), Markdown (https://www.daringfireball.net/projects/markdown/syntax), and other formats, which are transformed into HTML by the corresponding generators.

2. HtmlSC checks the generated HTML for broken links, missing images, and other semantic issues.

3. HtmlSC creates a test report that is similar to the well-known unit test report.

The following diagram depicts how **HtmlSC** operates:

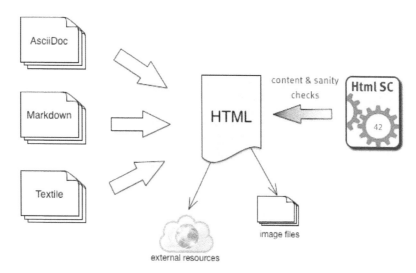

Figure 2.2: Semantic checking of HTML pages

Basic Usage

The usage of HtmlSC is explained as follows:

1. A user configures the location (directory and filename) of one or several HTML files and the corresponding images directory.

2. HtmlSC performs various checks on the HTML and reports its results either on the console or as an HTML report.

   HtmlSC can be run from the command line or as a Gradle plugin.

Basic Requirements

The requirements of HtmlSC are listed in the following table:

ID	Requirement	Explanation
G-1	Check HTML for semantic errors	HtmlSC checks HTML files for semantic errors, like broken links.
G-2	Gradle and Maven Plugin	HtmlSC can be run/used as Gradle and Maven plugin.
G-3	Multiple input files	Configurable for a set of files, processed in a single run, HtmlSC produces a joint report.
G-4	Suggestions	When HtmlSC detects errors, it shall identify suggestions or alternatives that might repair the error.
G-5	Configurable	Several features of checks shall be configurable, especially input files/location, output directory, timeouts and status-code behavior for checking external links etc.

Figure 2.3: Basic requirements

Required Checks

HtmlSC provides the following checks in HTML files:

Check	Explanation
Missing images	Check all image tags to see if the referenced image files exist.
Broken internal links	Check all internal links from anchor-tags ('href="#XYZ"') if the link targets "XYZ" are defined.
Missing local resources	Check if referenced files (e.g. css, js, pdf) are missing.
Duplicate link targets	Check all link targets (... id="XYZ") to see if the id's ("XYZ") are unique.
Malformed links	Check all links for syntactical correctness.
Illegal link targets	Check for malformed or illegal anchors (link targets).
Broken external links	Check external links for both syntax and availability.
Broken ImageMaps	Though ImageMaps are a rarely used HTML construct, HtmlSC shall identify the most common errors in their usage.

Figure 2.4: Required checks

1.2 Quality Goals

> **Note**
>
> You need to understand the quality goals (architecture goals) so that you can align your architecture and design decisions with these goals.
>
> These (usually long-term) quality goals diverge from the (usually short-term) goals of development projects. Keep these differences in mind!

The quality goals are as follows:

Priority	Quality Goal	Scenario
1	Correctness	Every broken internal link (cross reference) is found.
1	Correctness	Every potential semantic error is found and reported.
1	Safety	Content of the files to be checked is never altered. In case of doubt[18], report and let the user decide.
2	Flexibility	Multiple checking algorithms, report formats and clients. At least Gradle and command-line have to be supported.
2	Correctness	Correctness of every checker is automatically tested for positive AND negative cases.
3	Performance	Check of 100kB html file performed under 10 secs (excluding Gradle startup)

Figure 2.5: Quality goals

> **Note**
>
> Especially when checking external links, the correctness of links depends on external factors, such as network availability, latency, and server configuration, where HtmlSC cannot always identify the root cause of potential problems.

1.3 Stakeholders

> **Note**
>
> You want an overview of the persons, roles, or organizations that affect, are affected by, or can contribute to the system and its architecture. Make the concrete expectations of these stakeholders with respect to the architecture and its documentation explicit. Collect these in a simple table.

For our simple HtmlSC example, we have an extremely limited number of stakeholders. In real life, you will likely have many more stakeholders! Let's go over these here:

Role	Description	Goal / Intention
Documentation author	Writes documentation with HTML output	Wants to check that the resulting document contains good links, image references.
arc42 user	Uses arc42 for architecture documentation	Wants a small but practical example of how to apply arc42.
software developer		Wants an example of pragmatic architecture documentation

Figure.2.6: Stakeholders

II.2 Constraints

> **Note**
>
> You want to know the constraints that restrict your freedom regarding design decisions or the development process. Such constraints are often imposed by organizations across several IT systems.

HtmlSC should be:

- Platform-independent and should run on the major operating systems (Windows, Linux, and macOS).

- Implemented in Java or Groovy.

- Integrated with the Gradle build tool.

- Runnable from the command line.

- Have minimal runtime and installation dependencies (a Java runtime may be required to run HtmlSC).

- Developed under a liberal open source license. In addition, all the required dependencies/libraries need to be compatible with a Creative Commons license.

II.3 Context

You want to know the boundaries and scope of the system to distinguish it from neighboring systems. The context identifies the systems that have relevant external interfaces.

3.1 Business Context

> **Note**
>
> You want to identify all the neighboring systems and the different kinds of (business) data or events that are exchanged between your system and its neighbors.

The following table lists all the neighboring systems, along with a description of each:

Neighbor	Description
user	documents software with toolchain that generates html. Wants to ensure that links within this HTML are valid.
build system	mostly Gradle (https://gradle.org)
local HTML files	HtmlSC reads and parses local HTML files and performs sanity checks within those.
local image files	HtmlSC checks if linked images exist as (local) files.
external web resources	HtmlSC can be configured to optionally check for the existence of external web resources. Risk: Due to the nature of web systems and the involved remote network operations, this check might need significant time and might yield invalid results due to network and latency issues.

Figure 2.7: Business context

3.2 Deployment Context

> **Note**
>
> You will also want to know about the technical or physical infrastructure of your system, along with the physical channels or protocols.

The following diagram shows the participating computers (nodes) and their technical connections, along with the major artifact of HtmlSC, hsc-plugin-binary:

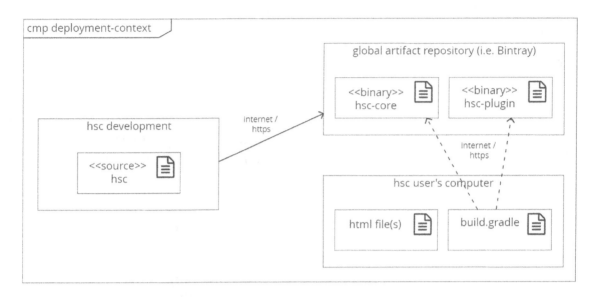

Figure 2.8: Deployment context

The following table explains the purpose of each node in hsc-plugin-library:

Node	Artifact Description
hsc-development	where development of HtmlSC takes place
hsc-plugin-binary	compiled and packaged version of HtmlSC including required dependencies
artifact repository	A global public cloud repository for binary artifacts, similar to MavenCentral (https://search.maven.org/), the Gradle Plugin Portal (https://plugins.gradle.com) or similar. HtmlSC binaries are uploaded to this server.
hsc user computer	where arbitrary documentation takes place with html as output formats.
build.gradle	Gradle build script configuring (among other things) the HtmlSC plugin to perform the HTML checking

Figure 2.9: Description of the components of the deployment context

II.4 Solution Strategy

> **Note**
>
> You need to provide a brief summary and explanation of the fundamental solution ideas and strategies. These key ideas should be familiar to everyone involved in the development and architecture process.
>
> Briefly explain how you achieve the most important quality requirements.

The following steps will explain the basics of the solution design:

1. Implement HtmlSC mostly in the Groovy programming language and partially in Java with minimal external dependencies.

2. We wrap this implementation into a Gradle plugin so that it can be used within automated builds. Details are given in the Gradle user guide (https://docs.gradle.org/current/userguide/userguide.html).The Maven plugin is still under development.

3. Apply the template method pattern (https://sourcemaking.com/design_patterns/template_method/) to enable multiple checking algorithms (see the concept of checking algorithms) and both HTML (file) and text (console) output.

4. Rely on standard Gradle and Groovy conventions for configuration and have a single configuration file. For the Maven plugin, this might lead to problems.

II.5 Building Block View

The building block view explains and divides the static decomposition of the system into building blocks (modules, components, subsystems, and packages) and their relationships. It shows the overall structure of the source code.

This view is organized in a top-down hierarchy.

5.1 HtmlSanityChecker (Whitebox)

The following diagram shows the whitebox:

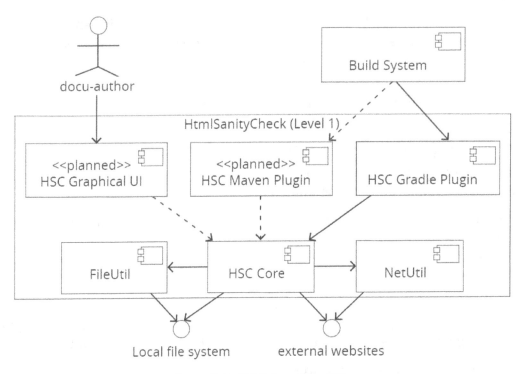

Figure 2.10: Whitebox (HtmlSC)

Rationale: We used *functional decomposition* to separate responsibilities:

- **HSC Core** will encapsulate checking logic and HTML parsing/processing.
- **Plugins** and **GraphicalUI** encapsulate all usage aspects

Contained Blackboxes

The following table shows the list of building blocks of HtmlSC whitebox:

Building Block	Description
HSC Core	HTML parsing and sanity checking
HSC Gradle Plugin	Exposes HtmlSC via a standard Gradle plugin, as described in the Gradle user guide (https://docs.gradle.org/current/userguide/userguide.html). Source: Package org.aim42.htmlsanitycheck, classes: HtmlSanityCheckPlugin and HtmlSanityCheckTask
NetUtil	package org.aim42.inet, checks for internet connectivity, configuration of http status codes
FileUtil	package org.aim42.filesystem, file extensions
HSC Graphical UI	(planned, not implemented)

Figure 2.11: Contained backboxes

5.2 Building Blocks – Level 2

5.2.1 HSC Core (Whitebox)

The following diagram shows the HSC Core (whitebox):

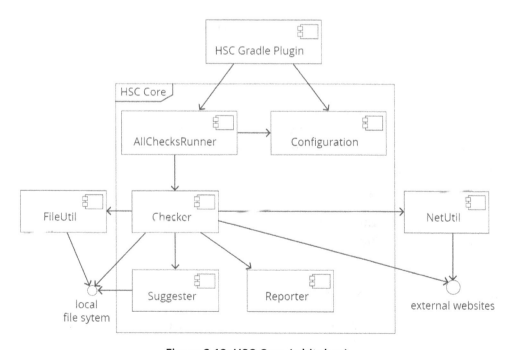

Figure 2.12: HSC-Core (whitebox)

The internal structure of HSC Core follows a functional decomposition, as follows:

- Configuration
- Parsing and handling HTML input
- Checking
- Creating suggestions
- Collecting the check's results

Contained Blackboxes

The following table describes the building blocks of contained blackboxes:

Building Block	Description
Checker	Contains the pure checking functionality. See its blackbox description below.
AllChecksRunner	Facade to the Checkers. Provides a (configurable) interface. Source: org.aim42.htmlsanitycheck. AllChecksRunner. Called by HSC GradlePlugin
Reporter	Reports checking results to either console or file.
Suggester	In case of checking issues, suggests alternatives (did you mean xyz?). Suggestions are included in results.

Figure 2.13: Contained backboxes

5.2.1.1 Checker (Blackbox)

The abstract **Checker** class provides the uniform interface (`public void check()`) to different checking algorithms.

Based on polymorphism, the actual checking is handled by subclasses of the abstract **Checker** class, which uses the template method pattern. It uses the concept of extensible checking algorithms.

5.2.1.2 Suggester (Blackbox)

For a given input (target), **Suggester** searches within a set of possible values (options) to find the **n** most similar values, for example:

- Target: "McDown".
- Options: {"McUp", "McDon", "Mickey"}.
- The resulting suggestion would be "McDon", because it has the greatest similarity to the target, "McDown".

This implementation is based on the Jaro-Winkler distance (https://en.wikipedia.org/wiki/Jaro%E2%80%93Winkler_distance), one of the algorithms that calculates the similarity between strings.

Suggester is used in the following cases:

- Broken image links: Compares the name of the missing image with all the available image filenames to find the closest match

- Missing cross references (broken internal links): Compares the broken link with all the available link targets (anchors)

Source: package org.aim42.htmlsanitycheck.suggest.Suggester

5.3 Building Blocks – Level 3

5.3.1 ResultsCollector (Whitebox)

The following diagram shows the whitebox for ResultsCollector:

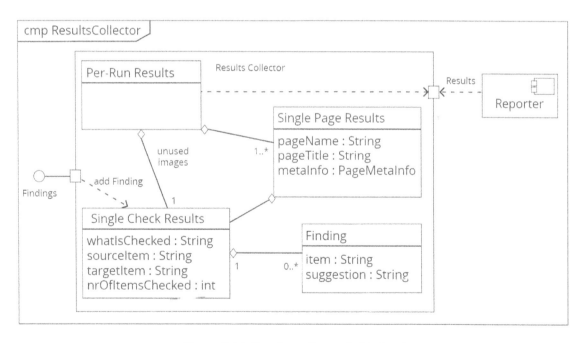

Figure 2.14: Results collector (whitebox)

The preceding structure follows the hierarchy of checks, managing results for the following:

- A number of pages/documents (**PerRunResults**)
- A single HTML page (**SinglePageResults**)
- The results of a single check, for example, **MissingImagesChecker** (**SingleCheckResults**)

Contained Blackboxes

The following table describes the building blocks of the **ResultsCollector** whitebox:

Building Block	Description
Per-Run Results	Aggregated results for potentially many HTML pages/documents.
SinglePageResults	Aggregated results for a single HTML page
SingleCheckResults	Results for a single type of check (e.g. missing -images check or broken-internal-link check)
Finding	A single finding, (e.g. "image 'logo.png' missing"). Can contain suggestions.

Figure 2.15: Contained backboxes

II.6 Runtime View

> **Note**
>
> The runtime view shows the behavior, interactions, and runtime dependencies of the building blocks in the form of concrete scenarios.
>
> This helps us understand how the building blocks of our systems fulfill their respective tasks at runtime, and how they communicate/interact with each other at runtime.

II.6.1 Executing All Checks

A typical scenario within HtmlSC is the execution of all the available checking algorithms on a set of HTML pages. The following diagram depicts the checking operation in HtmlSC:

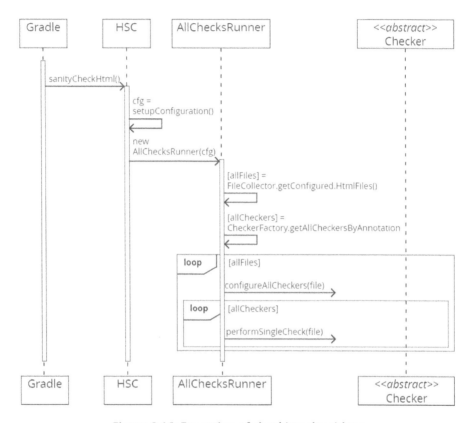

Figure 2.16: Execution of checking algorithms

The preceding diagram can be explained as follows:

1. The user or build calls the **htmlSanityCheck** build target.

2. Gradle (from within the build) calls **sanityCheckHtml.**

3. HSC configures the input files and output directory.

4. HSC creates an **AllChecksRunner** instance, gets all configured files into **allFiles** (planned), and gets all the available **Checker** classes based on the annotation.

5. Finally, it performs the checks, collecting the results.

II.6.2 Report Checking Results

The following diagram depicts the process of checking and reporting results in HtmlSC:

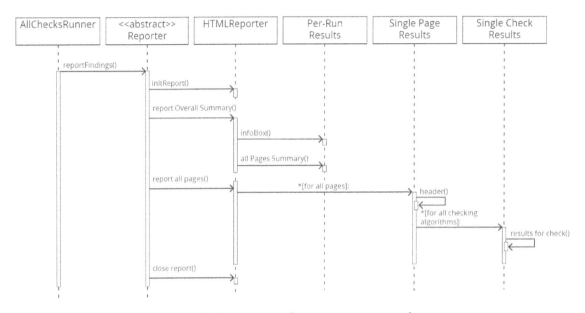

Figure 2.17: Sequence diagram – report results

Reporting is done in the natural hierarchy of results. Let's go through the steps:

1. Per "run" (**PerRunResults**): The date/time of this run is reported, files are checked, some configuration information, and a summary of results is prepared.

2. Per "page" (**SinglePageResults**):Create a page result header with a summary that includes the page name and results.

3. For each check that's performed on this page, create a section with **SingleCheckResults.**

4. Per "single check on this page," report the results for this particular check.

II.7 Deployment View

Note

You may like to know about the technical infrastructure where your system and its building blocks will be executed. This is especially important if your software is distributed or deployed on several different machines, application servers, or containers.

Sometimes, you need to know about different environments (such as dev, test, and production).

In large commercial or web systems, aspects such as scalability, clustering, automatic deployment, firewalls, and load balancing play important roles, which we definitely don't need for our small example.

The following figure depicts the HtmlSC deployment:

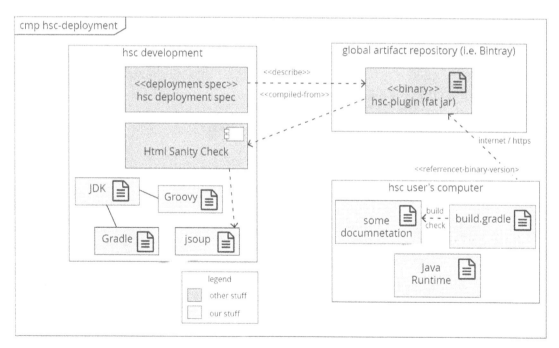

Figure 2.18: HtmlSC deployment (for use with Gradle)

The following table describes the different nodes of the HtmlSC deployment:

Node / Artifact	Description
hsc plugin binary	Compiled version of HtmlSC, including required dependencies.
hsc-development	Development environment
artifact repository	Global public cloud repository for binary artifacts, similar to mavenCentral (https://search.maven.org/) HtmlSC binaries are uploaded to this server.
hsc user computer	Where documentation is created and compiled to HTML.
build.gradle	Gradle build script configuring (among other things) the HtmlSC plugin.
build.gradle	Gradle build script configuring (among other things) the HtmlSC plugin.

Figure 2.19: Description of artifacts

The three nodes (*computers*) that are shown in the preceding diagram are connected via the internet.

Prerequisites

Let's go over some prerequisites:

- HtmlSC developers need the Java Development Kit, Groovy, Gradle, and the **JSoup** HTML parser.

- HtmlSC users need a Java runtime (> 1.6), plus a build file named **build.gradle**. See the following code for a complete example.

The following is an example **build.gradle** file:

```
buildscript {
repositories {
mavenLocal()
maven {
url "https://plugins.gradle.org/m2/"
    }
    }
```

```
dependencies {
// in case of mavenLocal(), the following line is valid:
classpath(group: 'org.aim42',

// in case of using the official Gradle plugin repository:
//classpath (group: 'gradle.plugin.org.aim42',
name: 'htmlSanityCheck', version: '1.0.0-RC-3')
    }
    }

plugins {
id 'org.asciidoctor.convert' version '1.5.8'
    }


// ==== path definitions =====
ext {
srcDir = "$projectDir/src/docs/asciidoc"

// location of images used in AsciiDoc documentation

srcImagesPath = "$srcDir/images"

// (input for htmlSanityCheck)
htmlOutputPath = "$buildDir"

    targetImagesPath = "$buildDir/images"
```

```
    }


    // ==== asciidoctor ==========
    apply plugin: 'org.asciidoctor.convert'


asciidoctor {
outputDir = file(buildDir)
sourceDir = file(srcDir)


sources {
include "many-errors.adoc", "no-errors.adoc"    }


attributes = [
doctype    : 'book',
icons    : 'font',
sectlink    : true,
sectanchors: true ]


resources {
from(srcImagesPath) { include '**' }
into "./images"    }
    }


    // ============================================================
    apply plugin: 'org.aim42.htmlSanityCheck'
```

```
    htmlSanityCheck {

// ensure asciidoctor->html runs first

// and images are copied to build directory

    dependsOn asciidoctor

    sourceDir = new File("${buildDir}/html5")

// files to check, in Set-notation
sourceDocuments = ["many-errors.html", "no-errors.html"]

// fail the build if any error is encountered
failOnErrors = false

// set the http connection timeout to 2 secs
httpConnectionTimeout = 2000

ignoreLocalHost = false
ignoreIPAddresses = false

    }

    defaultTasks 'htmlSanityCheck'
```

II.8 Crosscutting Concepts

One should explain crosscutting and the ubiquitous rules of the system. arc42 calls them concepts: they often affect multiple building blocks and are relevant in several parts of the system and its implementation. Examples include rules for the usage of technologies and/or frameworks and implementation rules, and the design or architecture patterns that are used.

8.1 Domain Model

The following diagram shows a domain model:

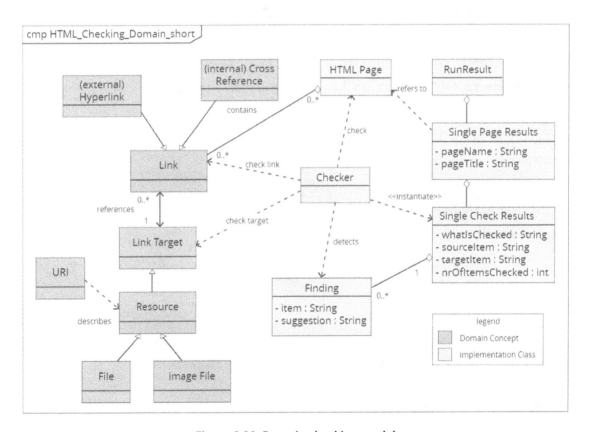

Figure 2.20: Domain checking model

The properties of the implementation classes are private since we manipulate them via getter/setter methods.

The following table describes every component of the domain model:

Term	Description
Anchor	HTML element to create ->Links. Contains link-target in the form <a href="link-target">
Cross Reference	Link from one part of the document to another part within the same document. Special form of ->Internal Link, with a ->Link Target in the same document.
External Link	Link to another page or resource at another domain.
Finding	Description of a problem found by one ->Checker within the ->HTML Page.
HTML Element	HTML pages (documents) are made up by HTML elements. For example:<a href="link target">, <img src="image.png">' and others. See the definition from the W3-Consortium (https://www.w3schools.com/html/html_elements.asp)
HTML Page	A single chunk of HTML, mostly regarded as a single file. Shall comply to standard HTML syntax. Minimal requirement: Our HTML parser can successfully parse this page. Contains ->HTML Elements. Synonym: HTML Document.
id	Identifier for a specific part of a document, for example: <h2 id="#someHeader">. Often used to describe ->Link Targets.
Internal Link	Link to another section of the same page or to another page of the same domain. Also called ->Cross Reference or Local Link.
Link	Any reference in the ->HTML Page that lets you display or activate another part of this document (->Internal Link) or, another document, image, or resource (can be either ->Internal (local) or ->External Link). Every link leads from the Link Source to the Link Target.
Link Target	Target of any ->Link, for example: heading or any other a part of ->HTML Documents, any internal or external resource (identified by URI). Expressed by ->id.
Local Resource	Local file, either other HTML files or other types like pdf, docx, and so on.
Run Result	The overall results of checking a number of pages (at least one page).
Single Page Result	A collection of all checks of a single ->HTML Page.
URI	Universal Resource Identifier. Defined in RFC-2396 (https://www.ietf.org/rfc/rfc2396.txt), the ultimate source of truth concerning link syntax and semantics

Figure 2.21: Description of the terms in the HTML domain checking model

8.2 Structure of HTML Links

For many web developers or HTML experts, the following information on URI syntax might be completely evident. We wrote this book for different kinds of people, so we included this information just in case.

HtmlSC performs various checks on HTML links (hyperlinks), which usually follow the URI syntax specified by RFC-2396 (https://www.ietf.org/rfc/rfc2396.txt). URIs are generally used to provide links to arbitrary resources (documents, files, or parts within documents).

Their general structure is depicted in the following diagram. A unit test follows:

[protocol://][host][:port][path][?query][#ref]

http://example.com:42/docs/index.html?name=aim42#INTRO

Figure 2.22: Generic URI structure

Test Showing Generic URI Syntax

The following code snippet is some test code for generic URI syntax:

```
@Test
public void testGenericURISyntax() {
// based upon an example from the Oracle(tm) Java tutorial:
// https://docs.oracle.com/javase/tutorial/networking/urls/urlInfo.\
html
def  aURL  =  new  URL(
"https://example.com:42/docs/tutorial/index.html?name=aim42#INT\
    RO");
    aURL.with  {
assert getProtocol() == "http"
assert getAuthority() == "example.com:42"
assert getHost() == "example.com"
```

```
assert getPort() == 42

assert getPath() == "/docs/tutorial/index.html"

assert getQuery() == "name=aim42"

assert getRef() == "INTRO"

    }

    }
```

8.3 Multiple Checking Algorithms

HtmlSC uses the template method pattern (https://sourcemaking.com/design patterns/template method/) to enable flexible checking algorithms:

"The Template Method defines *a skeleton of an algorithm* in an operation and defers some steps to subclasses."

We achieve this by defining the skeleton of the checking algorithm in one operation (**performCheck**), thereby deferring the specific checking algorithm steps to subclasses. The invariant steps are implemented in the abstract base class, while the variant checking algorithms have to be provided by the subclasses.

Template Method for Performing a Single Type of Check

```
    /**
 * Prerequisite: pageToCheck has been successfully parsed,
 * prior to constructing this Checker instance.
    **/
public CheckingResultsCollector performCheck() {
// assert prerequisite
assert  pageToCheck  !=  null
initResults()
return check() // subclass executes the actual checking algorithm
    }
```

The following diagram depicts the template method:

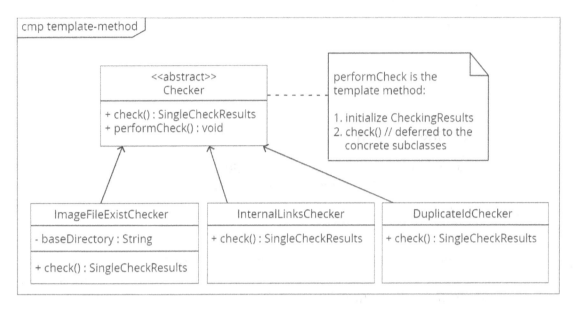

Figure 2.23: Template method (excerpt)

The following table describes the components of the template:

Component	Description
Checker	abstract base class, containing the template method check() plus the public method performCheck()
ImageFileExistChecker	checks if referenced local image files exist
InternalLinksChecker	checks if cross references (links referenced within the page) exist
DuplicateIdChecker	checks if any id has multiple definitions

Figure 2.24: Description of template components

8.4 Reporting

HtmlSC supports the following output (== `reporting`) formats and destinations:

- Formats include HTML and text.

- Destinations include file and console.

The reporting subsystem uses the template method pattern to allow different output formats (for example, the console and HTML). The overall structure of the reports is always the same.

Report Findings Using the Template Method Pattern

The (generic and abstract) reporting is implemented in the abstract **Reporter** class, as follows:

```
/**
 * main entry point for reporting - to be called when a report is requested
 * Uses template-method to delegate concrete implementations to subclasses
 */
public void reportFindings() {
initReport() // (1)
reportOverallSummary() // (2)
reportAllPages() // (3)
closeReport() // (4)
}
private void reportAllPages() {
 pageResults.each { pageResult ->
 reportPageSummary( pageResult ) // (5)
 pageResult.singleCheckResults.each { resultForOneCheck ->
 reportSingleCheckSummary( resultForOneCheck ) // (6)
 reportSingleCheckDetails( resultForOneCheck ) // (7)
 reportPageFooter()
 }
 }
```

The preceding code can be summarized as follows:

1. Initialize the report, that is, create and open the file, and copy the CSS, JavaScript, and image files.

2. Create the overall summary, along with the overall success percentage and a list of all checked pages with their success rates.

3. Iterate over all the pages.

4. Write a report footer. In the HTML report, also create a back-to-top link.

5. For a single page, report the number of checks and problems, plus the success rate.

6. For every **singleCheck** on that page, report a summary and all the detailed findings for a **singleCheck**.

7. For every checked page, create a footer, page break, or similar to graphically distinguish pages from each other.

The following sample report illustrates these steps:

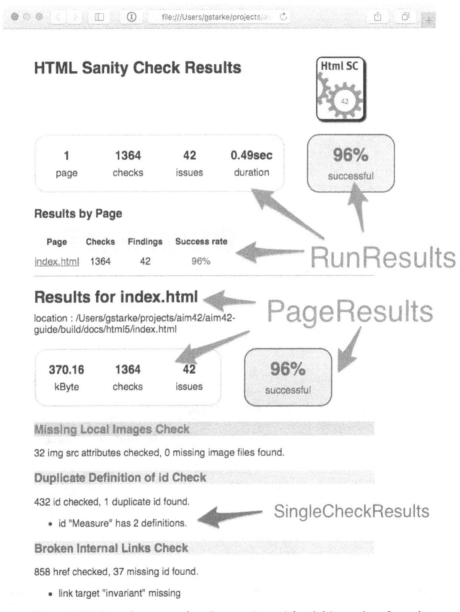

Figure 2.25: Sample report showing run/page/check hierarchy of results

II.9 Design Decisions

> **Note**
>
> You may like to understand some of the important, huge, expensive, risky, or otherwise special architecture and design decisions.
>
> It's especially interesting to understand the reasons for these decisions.

9.1 Checking of External Links Postponed

In the current version of HtmlSC, we can't check external links. These checks have been postponed for later versions.

9.2 HTML Parsing with jsoup

To check HTML, we parse it into an internal (DOM-like) representation. For this task, we use **jsoup** (https://jsoup.org), an open source parser without external dependencies.

To quote from their website:

"jsoup is a Java library for working with real-world HTML. It provides a very convenient API for extracting and manipulating data, using the best of DOM, CSS, and jQuery-like methods."

Goals of this decision: Check HTML programmatically by using an existing API that provides access and finder methods to the DOM tree of the file(s) to be checked.

Decision criteria would be as follows:

- Few dependencies, so the HtmlSC binary stays as small as possible
- Very easy to use: Simple and elegant (accessor and finder) methods to easily locate images, links, and link targets within the DOM tree
- Highly flexible: Can parse files and strings (and other) input

Alternatives to the HTML parser would be as follows:

- jsoup: A plain HTML parser without any dependencies and a rich API to access all the HTML elements in the DOM-like syntax. This is a clear winner!
- HTTPUnit: A testing framework for web applications and websites. Its main focus is web testing and it suffers from a large number of dependencies.
- HtmlCleaner (http://htmlcleaner.sourceforge.net/).

II.10 Quality Scenarios

> **Note**
>
> You may want to know about specific and operational quality requirements in the form of a specific quality tree. This section completes, augments, or refines the top-quality goals that were already given in arc42, section 1.2.

For our small example, such a quality tree is overly extensive, whereas in real-life systems, we've seen quality trees with more than 100 scenarios. Therefore, we will stick to (repeating) a few scenarios here.

Quality Scenarios

The quality scenarios are listed here:

Attribute	Description
Correctness	Every broken internal link will be found. Correctness Every missing (local) image will be found.
Correctness	Correctness of all checks is ensured by automated positive and negative tests.
Completeness	The results-report must contain all results (findings)
Flexibility	HtmlSC shall be extensible with new checking algorithms and new usage scenarios (i.e. from different build systems)
Safety	HtmlSC leaves its source files completely intact; Content of files to be checked will never be modified.
Performance	HtmlSC performs all checks on a 100kByte HTML file in less than 10 seconds.

Figure 2.26: Description of quality parameters

II.11 Risks and Technical Debt

> **Note**
>
> You may want to know about the technical risks of your system so that you can address potential future problems.
>
> In addition, you may want to support your management stakeholders (that is, project management, product owner, and so on) by identifying technical risks.

In our small example, we can't see any *real* risks for architecture and implementation. Therefore, the risks that follow are a bit artificial.

11.1 Technical Risks

The technical risks are as follows:

Risk	Description
Bottleneck with access rights on public repositories	Currently only one single developer has access rights to deploy new versions of HtmlSC on public servers like Bintray or Gradle plugin portal.
High effort required for new versions of Gradle	Upgrading Gradle from v-3.x to v-4.x required configuration changes in HtmlSC. Such effort might be needed again for future upgrades of the Gradle API.

Figure 2.27: Technical risks

11.2 Business or Domain Risks

The business risks are as follows:

Risk	Description
System might become obsolete	In case AsciiDoc or Markdown processors implement HTML checking natively, HtmlSC might become obsolete.

Figure 2.28: Business risks

II.12 Glossary

> **Note**
>
> You need to understand the most important domain terms and expressions that stakeholders use when communicating with the system, its interfaces, goals, and requirements.
>
> The glossary is one manifestation of our pledge to "explicit, not implicit," as it associates words or terms with sense, meaning, and semantics.

In the case of our small example, the terms given here should be good friends to most developers.

The following table lists the important terms that have been used throughout:

Term	Definition
Link	A reference within an →HTMLPage. Points to →LinkTarget
Cross Reference	Link from one part of a document to another part within the same document.
External Hyperlink	Link to another HTML-page or to a resource within another domain or site.
Run Result	Combined checking results for multiple pages (→HTMLPages)
SinglePageResults	Combined results of all Checker instances for a single HTML page.

Figure 2.29: Glossary of common terms

3

III - Mass Market Customer Relationship Management

By **Dr. Gernot Starke**

Mass Market Customer Relationship Management (**MaMa-CRM**) takes on the burden of (usually paper-based) customer contacts for organizations working in mass markets, such as insurance companies, credit card providers, mobile telecommunication providers, energy and water providers, and large real estate companies (in MaMa speak, these are called **Mandators**).

MaMa-CRM was initially ordered for an independent, mid-sized data center to support the launch of the German (government-enforced) e-Health card, which is now used to support campaigns such as telephone billing and electrical power metering.

For every mandator, there is at least one completely independent MaMa-CRM instance running, which is specifically configured for its mandator and a campaign.

The MaMa-CRM architecture documentation is quite heavy in terms of its requirements, describing several aspects of flexibility that triggered many central architecture decisions.

The team that built the system consisted of 7-10 people working in 2-4-week iterations for about 15 months.

I (Dr. Gernot Starke) had the honor of being part of that team in a responsible role. The original client allowed me to talk and write about the system without disclosing the company's name. I was not allowed to use any of the original documentation or source code.

Thanks to Thorsten, Sven, Arno, and others for their great cooperation.

III.1 Introduction and Requirements

This chapter describes the MaMa-CRM platform, a software-product family that coordinates processes between mass market service providers and their clients. MaMa-CRM provides the foundation for individual systems, which have to be customized or configured for specific CRM domains.

MaMa-CRM has been built and is being operated by an **Innovative DAta Center** (let's call it **InDAC**) – a company that provides a variety of hosted software services to its clients. Within business process outsourcing initiatives, InDAC is operating specific instances of MaMa-CRM for its customers.

Let's clarify MaMa-CRM's scope with a few brief examples (you'll find more details in the *Requirements Overview* section):

- Telecommunication providers offer new or updated tariffs to their customers. This is achieved through several possible channels, such as email, phone, letter, or fax, so that the service providers can respond or issue support queries regarding such offers.

- Retail organizations send specific advertising or marketing material to certain customers. Again, these can react to several different communication channels. These kinds of advertisements are part of target group marketing.

- Insurance companies propose modifications or enhancements for the existing contracts to specific customer groups. People who are insured, or organizations, can react over different communication channels, such as phone, mail, email, or even in person. If the consumers accept this proposal, they have to submit a legally binding signature.

Note

The real company behind the MaMa-CRM system prefers not to be disclosed here. The name "InDAC" is therefore pure fantasy. The original system wasn't called MaMa but had a different name – I hope you don't mind.

The following diagram shows a generalized overview of MaMa-CRM:

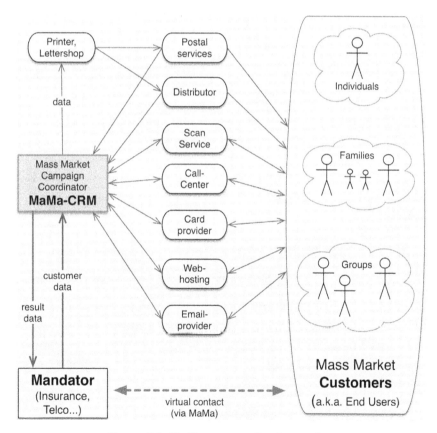

Figure 3.1: MaMa – generalized overview

In the preceding diagram, the **mandator** represents an arbitrary company or organization serving mass market customers. **MaMa**, our system, can host CRM campaigns for many different mandators from different industries.

1.1 Requirements Overview

MaMa-CRM controls customer relationship CRM campaigns, which InDAC (the contractor of MaMa) conducts for their mandators. InDAC's mandators are companies such as insurance or telco enterprises, which themselves offer services or products to mass market customers. These mandators outsource their CRM-related business processes to InDAC.

MaMa-CRM supports the following campaign types:

- Changes to tariffs or contracts for insurance companies, telecom and internet service providers, and energy suppliers. You'll find a detailed example of this process next.

- Processing of billing information for call-by-call telephone service providers: The mandator submits billing data to MaMa, which coordinates printing, submission, and support for the resulting invoices. The management or handling of payments is out of scope for MaMa-CRM.

- Management of binary images for credit card and insurance companies, which print the cardholders' images onto the cards to prevent misuse. The German e-Health card belongs in this category.

- Meter reading for either energy or water for companies or large-scale real estate enterprises.

As MaMa is the foundation for a whole family of CRM systems, it adapts to a variety of different input and output interfaces and channels without any source code modification needed!

1.1.1 Campaign Example: Mobile Phone Contract Modification

This example should clarify the complex business and technical requirements of MaMa.

MoPho is a (hypothetical) mobile phone provider with a large customer base and a variety of different tariff options (flat fee, time-based, volume-based, and so on). Some of these tariffs or tariff combinations are not marketable any more (a shorthand for **MoPho** does not earn its desired profit from them – but that's another story). Others are technically outdated.

In their ongoing effort to optimize their business, **MoPho**'s management decide to streamline their tariff landscape. Within a large campaign, they contact every customer with outdated tariffs and offer upgrades to new and mostly more beneficial tariff options. Some customers get to pay less but have to accept a longer contract duration. Others will have to pay a little more, but receive additional services such as increased capacity, bandwidth, or other benefits. When customers accept the new tariff offer, the formal contract between **MoPho** and the customer has to be updated, which requires a valid signature to be legally binding.

> ### Note
>
> In some countries, or for some contract types, there might be simpler solutions than a written signature. Please ignore this for the moment.

MoPho intends to inform certain customers via printed letters of the new tariff offerings. Customers can respond via letter, fax, phone, or in person at one of **MoPho**'s many sales outlets. As **MoPho**'s core competency involves phone services, they don't want to bother with printing letters, scanning and processing replies, answering phone inquiries, and dealing with other out of scope activities. Therefore, they employ MaMa-CRM as an all-around carefree solution. Look at the following MaMa approach to this scenario:

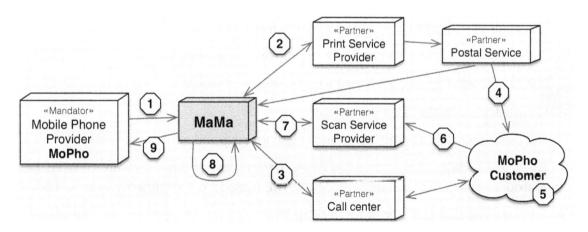

Figure 3.2: Telecommunication example scenario

The steps depicted in the preceding scenario need some explanation:

1. **MoPho** selects appropriate customers from its internal IT systems. We're talking about a 30+ million customer base, and approximately 10 million of those customers will be part of this campaign. **MoPho** exports their address, contract, and tariff data and transmits these to MaMa-CRM. **MaMa** imports this customer data.

2. **MaMa** forwards only the relevant parts of the customer data to the print service provider (a "**Partner**"). This company creates personalized letters from address and tariff data, prints those letters, and finally delivers them to the postal service (who ensures the letters finally end up in the customers' mailboxes).

3. MaMa now informs the call center (also a "**Partner**") participating in this campaign so that they can prepare for the customer's reaction.

4. In the meantime, the print service has delivered the letters to the postal service, which delivers letters to the respective customers. This is more difficult than it sounds: 1-5% of addresses tend to change within 12 months, depending on the customer base. Some customers refuse to accept marketing letters. The postal service informs MaMa about all these problem cases (address unknown, forwarding request, and so on) so that MaMa can decide on further action.

5. The customers decide what to do with the letter: There's a multitude of options here:

    The customer fills out the enclosed reply form and signs it.

    The customer fills out the reply form but forgets to sign it.

    The customer does not understand this offer and sends an inquiry by letter.

    The customer inquires by phone call.

    The customer ignores the letter and does not respond at all.

    There are additional special cases (the customer is not contractually capable, has a custodian or legal guardian, is underage, deceased, or temporarily unavailable).

    Let's assume that the customer accepts and sends the letter back via the postal service. These letters will be forwarded to the scan service provider (again, a "**Partner**"), which scans them and performs optical character recognition. **MaMa** imports the scan results from the scan service provider. Again, several cases are possible here. **MaMa** distinguishes between all possible cases and takes the appropriate actions:

    The form is completely filled and signed.

    The form is completely filled, but the customer forgot to sign it.

The customer signed it but forgot to fill in other important fields of the form.

If the form is not returned within an appropriate period of time, **MaMa** might decide to resend the letter, maybe with a different layout, wording, or even a different contractual offer.

Surely you can imagine several other possible options.

6. Finally, for every customer who accepted the changed tariff agreement, **MaMa** sends back the appropriate information so that the mandator of **MoPho** can internally change the corresponding master data, namely contracts and tariffs, and perform all the other required actions (activities in **MaMa**).

    For **MoPho**, the primary advantage of this is the centralized interface for all customer interaction: all the processes that are required to conduct this crucial campaign are handled by MaMa-CRM, without intervention by **MoPho**. Something else that's practical for **MoPho** is the nearly unlimited flexibility of MaMa-CRM to import and export a variety of different data formats. This flexibility allows MaMa-CRM to easily incorporate new campaign partners (such as a second scan service provider, an additional email service provider, or a web hosting partner).

1.1.2 Campaign Configuration

MaMa provides a software foundation for campaign instances that have to be extensively configured to operate for a specific mandator with a number of specific partners.

The following section provides an overview of such a configuration for the **MoPho** campaign we described in the previous section:

1. Configure the client master data:

    Define and configure the required data attributes and additional classes. Usually, this information is completely provided by the mandator.

    This data (for example, contract-, tariff-, offer-, and other business-specific entities or attributes) are modeled as extensions of the **MaMa** base model in UML.

    In the **MoPho** telecommunications example, this data includes the existing tariff, a list of potential new tariffs, the contract number, the validity period of the existing tariff, and the validity period of the new tariff.

2. Configure the required communication channels:

   Define and exchange security credentials (passwords, certificates, and user IDs).

   Determine the contact address, especially for handling technical and process issues.

3. Define the campaign metadata:

   This includes start and end dates, target dates for specific activities, the reply address for letters, the reply email address, and the phone number for the call center.

4. Define campaign activities:

   Campaign activities can be either input, output, or **MaMa** internal activities.

   Output activities *export* data to partners or the mandator, for example, `PrintLetter`, `DataToCallCenter`, `0044ataToScanServiceProvider`, `ResultsToMandator`, and `ProductionOrderToCardProvider`.

   Input activities *import* data provided by the mandator or partners, for example, `MasterDataFromMandatorImport`, `ScanDataImport`, `CallCenterImport`, and `SalesOutletImport`.

   Internal activities define data maintenance operations, for example, to delete customer data 60 days after completion and delete all campaign data 120 days after campaign termination.

5. Model campaign flow:

   The required flow of activities, that is, what needs to happen under which conditions (including plausibility checks).

1.1.3 Activities Subject to Charge

Some activities result in charges, such as the following:

- Sending letters via a postal service results in postal charges.
- Producing e-Health cards results in card production charges.

Since we are talking about potentially millions of client activities, these charges will amount to a significant flow of money:

MaMa-CRM does NOT handle billing and payment processes.

Instead, these are handled in parallel with MaMa campaigns by InDAC's finance department.

> **Note**
>
> In the real system, billing and payment were usually processed by the mandators (!), but these third-party processes are not significant for the software architecture, and therefore are left out of this documentation.

1.1.4 Additional Requirements

This section will describe the additional requirements as follows:

Status and Financial Reporting

MaMa has to create campaign reports containing all campaign activities and their results (for example, how many letters were printed, how many calls from clients were processed in the call center, how many clients sent their return letter, and so on).

It's especially important to report activities subject to a charge (having financial consequences). Although MaMa-CRM is not responsible for the resulting billing and payment processes, mandators and partners need reliable and trustworthy reports about such activities.

MaMa offers adequate standard reports that cover these cases.

Client Data Belongs to Mandators

MaMa-CRM follows a very strict data protection policy: all the data processes in campaigns are somehow related to the clients and need to be kept strictly confidential. Mandators always remain owners of all such data, from whatever partner it is transferred to and by whatever activities.

After a campaign officially ends, all the data, including backups, configurations, data, and metadata needs to be deleted.

> **Note**
>
> Effectively, this requirement forbade the use of the well-known version control systems **SubVersioN** (**SVN**), as, by the development time of MaMa-CRM, SVN could not reliably *purge* files from its version history!
>
> Therefore, a campaign spanning the SVN repository was not allowed.

1.2 Quality Goals

The quality goals are listed as follows:

1.2.1 Flexibility First

The following diagram illustrates the important aspects of flexibility:

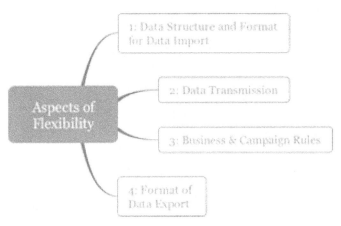

Figure 3.3: Aspects of flexibility

Simply put, **MaMa** is a data hub with flexibility in several aspects: it imports data (**aspect 1**) coming over various transmission channels (**aspect 2**) and executes a set of specific business rules (**aspect 3**) to determine further activities to be performed with this data. Such activities consist of data exports (**aspect 4**) to certain business partners (such as print, scan, or fax service providers, call centers, and so on).

MaMa has to be flexible in terms of these aspects.

Aspect 1: Flexibility in Data Structure and Format:

MaMa always deals with variants of client data – the simplest version could look like an instance of the following class definition:

```
public class Client
String primaryKey
String lastName
String firstName
Date birthDate
String title
Address postalAddress
```

MaMa needs to import such data from various campaign partners. These partners operate their own IT systems with their own data formats. They will export the affected data records to a format of their choice. **MaMa** needs to handle many such formats:

- **Comma-separated values** (**CSV**): Attributes are separated by a (configurable) delimiter, for example, "id01," "starke," "gernot," "23-jul-1963," "willi-lauf," "D-50858," "cologne," and "germany."

- The field order and delimiter can vary.

- Elements can be enclosed in either " or " or even "".

- Fixed length formats, where every data record has a fixed length. Shorter entries are padded with empty strings or zeros.

- XML dialects, either conforming to an appropriate schema or **Document Type Definition** (**DTD**).

Regardless of the format, data elements need to comply with validation or plausibility rules. The good news is that no serialized objects from programming language runtimes (for example, from a Java virtual machine) have to be processed.

Aspect 2: Flexibility in Transmission Formats and Modes

MaMa needs to handle the following transmission-related aspects:

- Standard transmission protocols (FTP, SFTP, HTTP, and HTTPS) as both client and the server.

- Compression

- Encryption

- The creation of checksums, at least with counters, MD5, and SHA-1.

- Mandator- or campaign-specific credentials for secure transmissions.

- Transmission metadata, that is, to count the number of successful transmissions and send the number of the last successful transmission as a prefix to the next transmission.

Aspect 3: Flexibility in Business/Campaign Rules

MaMa needs to support several categories of campaign rules (sometimes called business rules), as follows:

- What are the required and possible activities in this campaign?

- In what order shall these activities be executed?

- Certain types of activities (especially data import activities) are sometimes triggered by **Partner** organizations. What kind of event triggers what activities?

- How often should we remind clients/customers by letter?

- When should we call clients/customers by phone?

- What data is mandatory from the customer and what is optional?

- How long should we keep data records and when should we delete or archive data records?

- Who should we contact when certain (data) conditions arise?

Aspect 4: Flexibility in Data Export

Now that **MaMa** has received and processed data (by import, transmission, and rule processing), it needs to send data to the campaign partners. Analogous to data imports, these receiving partners have very specific requirements concerning data formats.

It is pretty common for **MaMa** to receive data from a partner company or mandator in CSV format, import it into its own relational database, process it record by record, and export some records in XML to one partner and some other records in a fixed format to another partner.

1.2.2 Quality Goals (Scenarios)

The following are the various scenarios for quality goals as described previously:

Prio 1: Flexibility

MaMa-CRM can do the following:

- Import and export (configurable) CSV and fix-record-length data.

- Import and export data via FTP, SFTP, HTTP, and HTTPS as the client and server.

- Handle compressed data. A compression algorithm is configurable per activity, while standard lossless compression has to be supported.

- Handle encrypted data. Security credentials need to be exchanged between parties prior to campaigns during the campaign's setup. **Pretty Good Privacy** (**PGP**) or derivatives are recommended.

- Handle hashes or similar transmission metadata, which is configurable per campaign.

    For all of these topics, InDAC administrators can fully configure all campaign-specific aspects within one workday.

Prio 2: Security

MaMa will keep all its client and campaign-related data safe. It will never be possible for campaign-external parties to access data or metadata.

InDAC administrators need to sign nondisclosure contracts to be allowed to administer campaign data. This organizational issue is out of scope for MaMa.

Prio 3: Runtime Performance

MaMa can fully process 250,000 scanned return letters within 24 hours.

1.2.3 Non-goals (out of scope) are listed as follows:

- MaMa shall be exclusively operated by InDAC. It shall not evolve into a marketable product.

- MaMa shall not replace conventional CRM systems, such as Siebel™, salesforce.com, or others.

- MaMa does not handle the billing and payment of any charges that are generated by its activities, for example, sending letters and so on.

1.3 Stakeholder

The following table explains the importance of every stakeholder:

Role	Description	Goal, Intention
Mandator	The organizations paying InDAC for conducting one or more campaigns	Minimal effort to get data into and out of MaMa-CRM, minimal effort to configure campaign rules etc.
Management of contractee (InDAC)	Requires flexible and performant foundation for current and future business segments.	Periodical cooperation on current and changed requirements, solution approaches.
Software developers participating in MaMa implementation	Design MaMa internal structure, implement building blocks.	Active participation in technical decisions.
Partner	Companies supporting parts of the campaign processes, like print- or scan service providers, postal service, card producers, call centers. Partner need to send and receive data from MaMa, need to negotiate interface contracts, organizational and operational details.	Effective, productive and robust interfaces between MaMa and partner.
Government Agency	Several agencies regulate MaMa campaigns, for example: insurance regulation body or governmental IT-security body.	Ensure that MaMa fulfills all data security regulations.
Eclipse-RCP (rich client platform)	Open source project (provider of UI framework)	MaMa uses Eclipse rich client platform to implement the graphicaluser interface. Eclipse changes its API quite often and therefore (unpredictably) influences UI development.

Figure 3.4: A table of Stakeholders

1.3.1 Special Case: German e-Health Card

The following diagram shows a example of a German e-Health card:

Figure 3.5: Sample German e-Health card

InDAC hosted several campaigns in the evaluation phase of the German e-Health card, which had to comply with business and technical standards issued by the corresponding standardization body. A company was founded just for this purpose by the German government. An interesting fact about the MaMa-CRM development team is that company wasn't operational when **MaMa** development started, and so the standards that had to be adhered to hadn't even been created or published.

1.3.2 Partner or Mandator-Specific Interface Details

MaMa-CRM offers detailed interface specification documents, which partners (such as print or scan service providers) can use to implement, configure, and operate their interfaces in MaMa. Due to MaMa's great flexibility, it usually works the other way round: **Mandators** and **Partners** provide MaMa with their interface descriptions, which MaMa administrators only configure to make operational.

III.2 Constraints

The following are the constraints for MaMa:

General Constraints

The general constraints for MaMa are as follows:

- Set up a campaign without programming:

- To set up a campaign, no *programming* is necessary. *Configuration* in various forms is allowed.

- Implementation based on Java:

- MaMa-CRM works on a recent Java runtime (>1.6).

- Use Oracle as a database:

  The InDAC holding company has negotiated a favorable deal with Oracle Inc. in terms of license and maintenance fees. Therefore, Oracle DB has to be used for data storage.

Software Infrastructure Constraints

The software-related constraints are as follows:

- Linux operating system (preferably Red Hat Enterprise Linux as hardened editions certified by several security organizations exist).

- Open source frameworks with liberal licenses are possible (GNU and FSF licenses not allowed).

- Code generation/ **Model Driven Software Development** (**MDSD**) preferred for development.

- Use of the UML modeling tool recommended.

- InDAC prefers iterative development processes but does not impose them.

- Sound technical documentation: InDAC emphasizes long-lasting, robust, and cost-effective software systems, and therefore strongly requires maintainable, understandable, and expressive technical documentation (part of which you are currently reading).

Operational Constraints

The operational constraints are as follows:

- Every MaMa-CRM instance shall be operable in its own virtual machine.

- MaMa shall run in batch/background mode to minimize operational overhead.

- Complete configuration shall be possible from a custom Eclipse plugin (alternatively, we can do this via a browser).

III.3 Context

The following are the different contexts that influenec MaMa:

3.1 (Generic) Business Context

Every MaMa instance communicates with a single mandator and one or more partner organizations, as shown in the following diagram. Partners are external service providers, for example, printer services, mail delivery services, scan services, and call center or internet hosting providers. Consider the following diagram:

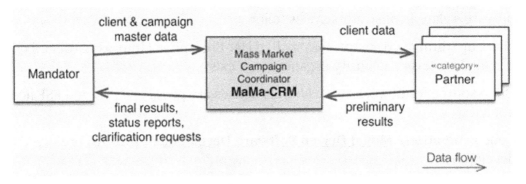

Figure 3.6: MaMa generic business context (informal)

Client data (outbound)

Client data is sent to partners on a "need-to-know" basis to achieve data minimality: every partner organization only gets the data they absolutely require for fulfilling their campaign tasks.

For example, **MaMa** will not disclose a client's street address to call centers (they usually get to know the name, phone number, and sometimes one or two additional attributes for verification purposes).

On the other hand, print service providers usually don't get to know the phone numbers of clients, as the latter is not required for delivering printed letters via postal services.

3.1.1 Formal Business Context

The following diagram provides a more formal version of the context diagram. It includes an admin interface, which was left out in the informal version:

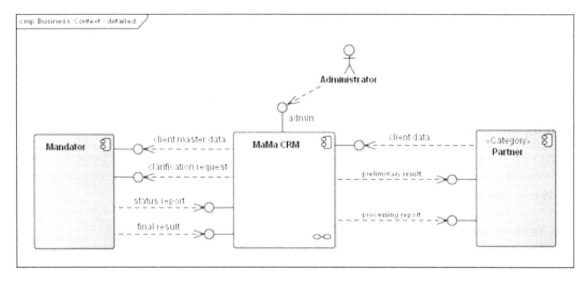

Figure 3.7: MaMa generic business context (formal)

The admin interface allows **MaMa** and campaign administrators to perform all the required administrative tasks that are needed to initialize, configure, and operate campaigns.

3.1.2 Specific Business Context: Mobile Phone Contract Modification

The following diagram details the example we looked at previously:

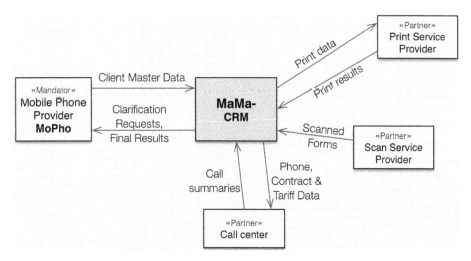

Figure 3.8: Mobile phone example context

The data flows are detailed (in excerpts) in the following table:

Neighbor system	Exchanged Data	Format
Mandator (inbound)	Client Master Data: Name, Address, Contact, Contract, Tariff. Once for every client in the campaign, second as response to clarification requests.	Zip-compressed CSV, via sftp (mandator uploads)
Mandator (outbound)	Final results: ID, tariff and contract details for every client who accepted the contract modification proposal	Zip-compressed CSV over sftp, MaMa uploads
Mandator (outbound)	Clarification request	—– " —–
"Print Service Provider (outbound)"	Print Data: Name, Address, parts of contract and tariff.	Zip-compressed, PGP-encrypted CSV via http upload

Figure 3.9: Context details for the mobile phone contract modification campaign

Mapping Attributes to CSV Fields

For every instance of MaMa, the mapping of data attributes to fields/records in data transmissions has to be specified in detail. This is done by a domain-specific language; details are described in the CSV *Import/Export* section.

3.1.2 Technical/Deployment Context

MaMa instances are supposed to run distinct virtual machines (whereas certain mandators or campaigns require instances to be deployed on their own physical hardware, which results in significantly higher campaign costs).

> **Note**
>
> Some mandators with extremely high security requirements negotiated their own distinct physical hardware for their MaMa instance(s).

The following diagram provides a schematic overview of the typical **MaMa** deployment setup:

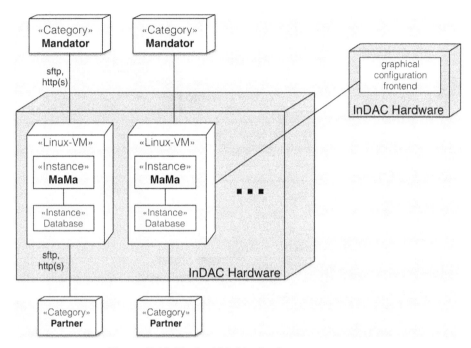

Figure 3.10: Typical MaMa deployment context

The following table describes each element of the MaMa deployment setup:

Element	Description
«Instance» MaMa	A distinct instance of MaMa, running a specific campaign (connected to a single mandator and a number of campaign-specific partner organizations)
InDAC Hardware	Physical server (Dell, HP or similar), located on InDAC premises. Running RHE Linux and a virtualization environment (not shown in diagram)
«Category» Mandator	For every MaMa instance there is one distinct mandator.
«Category» Partner	For every MaMa instance there might be several different partner organizations, each one having a distinct communication channel.
«Instance» Database	Every MaMa instance has its own database instance, usually within the same virtual machine.
Linux VM	Virtualized (RHE) Linux environment. Configured to disallow unwanted external access (e.g. ssh only allowed from within InDAC)

Figure 3.11: Description of the elements of MaMa deployment

III.4 Solution Strategy

Here, we will just find the shorthand form of the architectural approaches for the most important (quality) requirements, as well as links to the appropriate cross cutting concepts.

Goal/Requirement	Architectural Approach	Details
Flexible Data Structure	Database structure + persistence code is completely (100%) generated from UML-model	Section 8.1
Flexibility in Transmission Formats (CSV and fix-record-formats)	Create domain-specific languages for CSV and fix-format import/export configurations. Build an ANTLR based parser for these languages plus the corresponding interpreters.	Section 8.2
Flexibility (Configurable CSV/fix formats)	Implement customized editor for CSV/fix DSL as Eclipse plugin	Section 8.2
Performance (import/process 250k images/24hrs)	Treat images as special case, store images in filesystem instead of database, create unique path/filename based upon cient-ID, include load-testing in automatic build, create test-data generator	Include special case for image persistence in code generator, Section 8.1

Figure 3.12: Goals for solution strategy

III.5 Building Blocks

This section describes each building block of the deployment setup:

5.1 MaMa Whitebox Level 1

The following figure depicts the structure of MaMa whitebox:

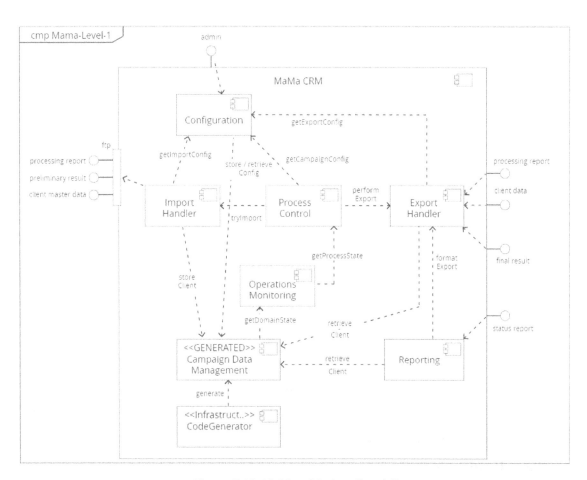

Figure 3.13: MaMa whitebox (level 1)

The structure of building blocks within MaMa is based on *functional decomposition* and the concept of *generated persistence*.

It contains the following components:

Element	Description
Import Handler	Imports data from Partners or Mandator via external interfaces
Export Handler	Exports data to Partners or Mandator via external interfaces
Configuration	Maintains configuration of all import- and export activity types, import- and export filters and campaign business rules. Includes syntax driven editors for configuration.
Reporting	Reports campaign state to Mandator and Partners, as configured.
Process Control	Responsible for management and execution processes within a campaign, especially for execution of campaign specific business rules.
Campaign Data Management	Completely generated. Stores all client- and campaign data.
Operations Monitoring	Monitors (and reports) all import and export processes plus database and application state.
Code Generator	Generates the (complete) CampaignDataManagement from a campaign specific UML model. See persistence concept for details.

Figure 3.14: Components of MaMa Whitebox Level 1

Import Handler (Blackbox):

The **Import Handler** contains the core functions to import data from partners or mandators via external interfaces. It handles CSV, fixed format, or XML input, either encrypted or compressed (or both) into a configurable structure.

The following are the interfaces:

Interface (From-To)	Description
getImportConfig	Read all required configuration information to perform imports, especially details about data structures (like csv formats) and filter chains.
storeClient	Sends an imported instance of Client to CampaignDataManagement to be either updated or inserted.
tryImport (from ProcessControl)	ProcessControl either calls or schedules a specific imports activity.
ImportHandler -> external port	ImportHandler needs to access various external entities, like ftp server, file system or even remote access to Mandator or Partner hosts.

Figure 3.15: Import Handler interfaces

Quality of Service:

Import Handler implements extensive failure handling mechanisms and can, therefore, deal with a large number of error categories (for example, communication errors, data format errors, compression and encryption issues, and so on).

For details, see the *Import Handler (Whitebox)* section.

Configuration (Blackbox)

Configuration is responsible for providing deploy-time flexibility to all MaMa subsystems. It handles the following kinds of configuration information:

- Data import and export configuration, which consists of CSV, fix-format, and XML formats, transmission and routing information, endpoints, network configuration, configuration for compression, encryption, and similar filter operations, and account and security information that's required for MaMa to communicate with the campaign-specific external systems.

- Campaign configuration, which consists of validation rules and activities that indicate what kind of imports, exports, and maintenance activities are required for this campaign.

- Configuration for archiving imported data.

Interfaces:

- For all configuration methods, **campaignID** and **mandatorID** always need to be input parameters.

- Configuration information is always a subclass of the (abstract) superclass configuration. Let's go over these now:

Interface (From-To)	Description
getImportConfig	Methods to get import configurations for a specific campaign.
getExportConfig	Methods to get export configurations for a specific campaign.
getCampaignConfig	
store/retrieveConfig	Calls DataManagement to store/retrieve configuration data.

Figure 3.16: Interfaces for Configuration (Blackbox)

The quality of service is not documented.

MaMa Whitebox Level 2

This section describes the components of MaMa level 2 as follows:

Import Handler (Whitebox):

The following figure depicts the import handler of MaMa level 2:

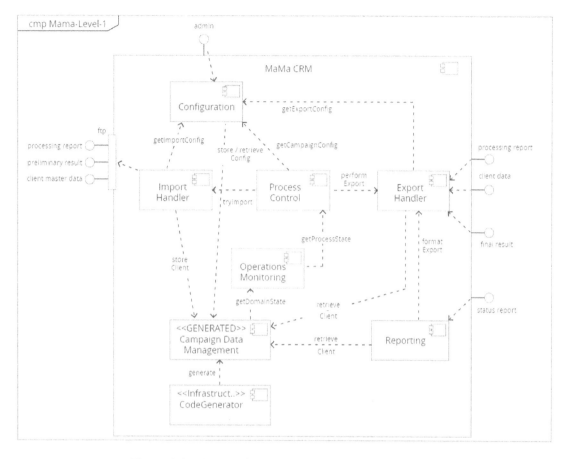

Figure 3.17: Composite structure of the Import Handler

This is (again) based on the *functional decomposition* of the generic import process. It contains the following black boxes:

Element	Description
Receiver	Receives data from partners or mandators via the ImportData port.
ImportErrorHandler	Handles the various possible errors during import. With severe errors, import is stopped. Many (especially record or object level) errors are recoverable - these will be logged, eventually the administrator is notified.
ImportData (Port)	Connection to the outside world - via ftp and http, usually transmitted via VPN.
FileArchiver	Non-erasable archive where all imported files are kept for auditability.
FileFilter	Various filter operations, like decrypt, unzip etc. Explained in the filter concept in section 8
Validator	Checks files, records (collections of strings) and client objects for validity.
UnMarshaller	Creates Java objects from collections of strings by using reflection magic. You don't want to know all the dirty details of this component.

Figure 3.18: Import Handler interfaces for MaMa whitebox Level 2

The interfaces are not documented.

MaMa Whitebox Level 3

The following figure depicts the MaMa level 3 setup:

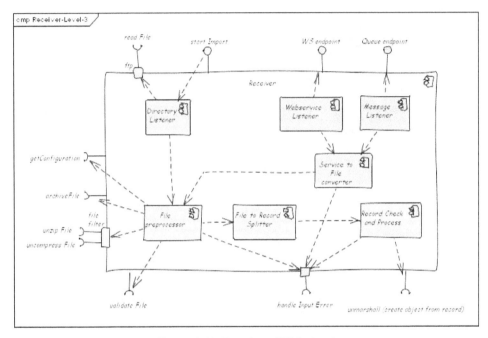

Figure 3.19: Receiver (Whitebox)

We have to admit that this structure just evolved out of a number of prototypes. A more functional oriented design would most likely improve understandability, but we never refactored the code in that direction due to different priorities.

It contains the following black boxes:

Element	Description
{Directory | WebServicer | Message}Listener	Components that listen for input of specific kinds, e.g. the DirectoryListener watches for new files to appear in certain directories, (configurable) either in a local or remote file system.
FileProcessor	Completely handles input files, calls all required operations to be performed on the file (archive, unzip, decrypt etc.). A big mess of spaghetti code - you don't want to look at it...
FileToRecordSplitter	Depending on configuration, creates a collection of records from the imported file. Most often a record is represented by a single row/line within the file, but sometimes several lines from the file have to be combined.

Figure 3.20: Elements in the receiver whitebox

III.6 Runtime View

This section focuses on the description of Runtime View.

6.1 Import File

One of the major use cases is *Import File*, which can be from both the mandator and partner. Such files always contain client-related data in configurable formats (CSV, fix-formats, or XML).

We will split the explanation of *import file* into two phases:

1. Import a raw generic file (from an external source).

2. Validate the imported data and update the internal client database.

6.1.1 Import Raw Generic File

First, we will explain the generic import, where no campaign-specific activities are executed. This concerns the **configureReceiveChannel** and **instantiateFilterChain()** activities:

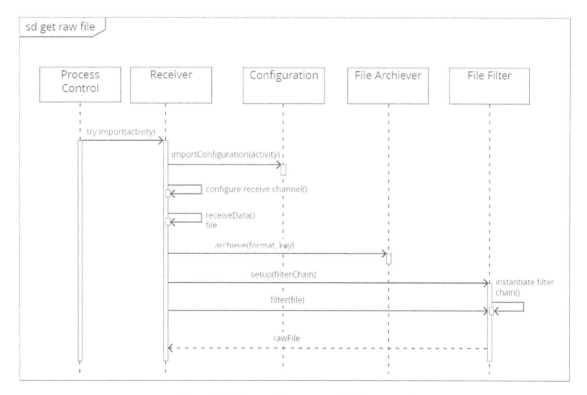

Figure 3.21: Importing a raw file (first part)

The process of importing raw files can be described as follows:

1. **tryImport ProcessControl** starts the import. The activity is a unique ID identifying the mandator, the campaign, and the activity.

2. **importConfiguration** gets all the required configuration information.

3. **configureReceiveChannel** prepares everything that's needed to get data from an external source. For example, URLs, filenames, and authentication credentials for an external FTP server need to be configured here.

4. The archive sends the file to the (configured) archive system, usually an optical write-once non-erasable backup archive.

5. **setup** initializes the required filters, for example, **unzip** or **decrypt**.

6. **filter** executes all the filters

Steps 5 and 6 are a dynamically configured pipe-and-filter dataflow subsystem. We will talk about the filter concept in more detail later.

6.1.2 Validate File

In terms of prerequisites, the data needs to be imported from an external source and successfully filtered (that is, decrypted and decompressed). See the previous section for more information.

The following diagram contains error handling. In successful cases, there will be no errors. Calls to **ImportErrorHandler** are only executed if errors occur:

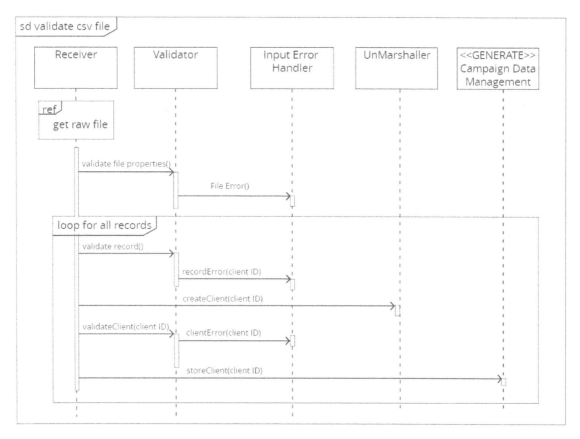

Figure 3.22: Validating the imported data (the second part of data import)

III.7 Deployment View

This section focuses on describing the Deployment View setup.

7.1 Deployment Overview

It was a longstanding goal of MaMa to deploy and operate each MaMa campaign on a dedicated virtual machine in order to clearly separate mandator-specific data from other instances.

The operating system-level configuration and operation mode of these virtual machines and their host machine directly influences the level of security the campaigns have. These topics have to be the subject of regular security inspections and reviews.

> **Note**
>
> Due to the sensitive nature of the data that was handled by the original MaMa system, the owner required strict nondisclosure in that aspect. Therefore, we are not allowed to go into any detail regarding security.

The following figure depicts an overview of the MaMa deployment:

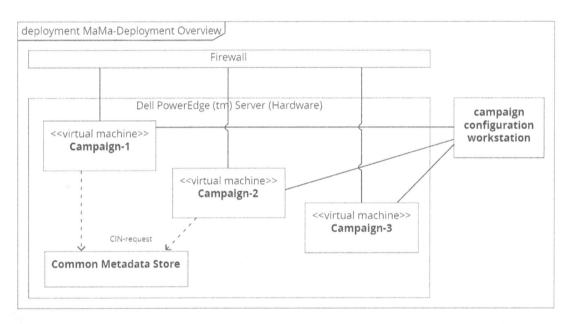

Figure 3.23: MaMa Deployment Overview

The following table describes the components of the MaMa deployment:

Element	Description
Campaign-i	Virtual machine for one single campaign.
Common Metadata	Store Used only in eHealth campaigns to synchronize generation of CIN IDs (see below)
Campaign Configuration Workstation	Workstation (standard PC running Java-enabled OS) used to configure campaigns.
CIN request	Request for Common Insurance Number (see below)

Figure 3.24: Elements of MaMa deployment

7.2 Campaign-Specific Virtual Machine

For every campaign that's operated by InDAC, there will be a single dedicated virtual machine containing a database instance and all the required MaMa code (except the graphical configuration UI).

7.3 Common Metadata Store (CoMeS)

The German government regulations for the e-Health card contained a very specific process to generate the **Common Insurance ID** (**CID**) for people. This ID could only be generated by a single government entity (formerly the GPFunds, "Deutsche Rentenanstalt." Since 2012, they are known as the ISTG: https://de.wikipedia.org/wiki/ Informationstechnische_Servicestelle_der_gesetzlichen_Krankenversicherung).

Requests for calculating the 10-digit CID have to be wrapped in a request envelope

containing the following metadata:

- The unique ID of the requesting entity (usually the tax ID number of the organization/company issuing the request). MaMa needed to use the tax ID of the InDAC data center.

- Request purpose (for MaMa, this is a constant).

- **Request sequence number** (**RSN**).

This RSN needed to be an uninterrupted sequence of numbers as GPFunds wanted to make sure it did not miss any requests. For MaMa, this implied the need for a synchronization mechanism between otherwise independent virtual machines. We decided to implement the Common Metadata Store for this reason.

For security reasons, MaMa did not use a real database and instead used a custom-built synchronization solution.

7.4 Campaign Configuration Machine

One (or several) operator workstations (standard PCs) will be used to configure MaMa instances after they have been physically deployed on their respective virtual machines.

The configuration UI is built as an Eclipse RCP (**Rich Client Platform**) plugin.

III.8 Cross cutting Concepts

This section will describe the various technical and related concepts of MaMa deployment:

8.1 Generated Persistence Based on the Domain Model

MaMa uses a code generator to generate all required persistence code from a UML entity model. The overall concept of this generation is depicted in the following diagram. Generic and campaign-specific parts are stereotyped in this diagram. The

"campaign-specific" Data Management component is automatically created and packaged by the build process:

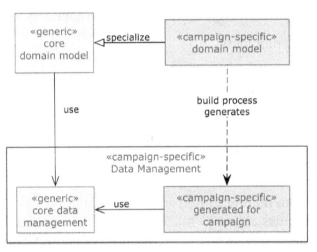

Figure 3.25: Overview of code generation

The following table describes the various elements of the code generation setup:

Element	Applicability	Description
Core Domain Model	«generic»	UML model containing the generic classes and relations every MaMa instance needs.
Core Domain Data Management	«campaign-specific»	Handwritten code, some Hibernate stuff, some generic finder and repository methods.
Specific Domain Model	«campaign-specific»	UML model enhancing the Core Domain Model.
Data Management	«campaign-specific»	Java jar archive generated by the code generator specifically for a campaign. Name and ID of campaign is contained in metadata, so different instances of this element are distinguishable, e.g. for audit or revision purposes.
Code Generator	«generic»	not shown in diagram.

Figure 3.26: Element of code generation setup

This concept relies on a number of prerequisites.

Prerequisites

These are as follows:

- Every MaMa instance will handle data related to individual people, known as *clients* in MaMa domain terminology.

- All the clients will have a small number of common attributes.

- For all productive campaigns, MaMa needs to handle an arbitrary number of additional attributes.

- Every mandator will add several campaign-specific attributes to the client, and/or will add campaign-specific types (such as insurance contracts or mobile and phone contracts).

- Once configured prior to the campaign's start, these campaign-specific data structures will rarely change.

> **Note**
>
> In several years of the MaMa operation, data structures within an active campaign always remained fixed. Therefore, MaMa never needed any data migration utilities.

8.1.1 Generic Domain Model (MaMa-Core-Domain)

The following figure depicts the general model of the MaMa domain:

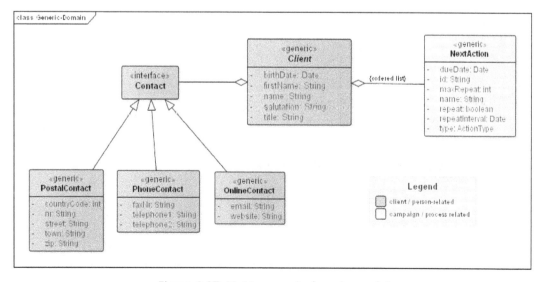

Figure 3.27: MaMa generic domain model

The following table describes every element of the MaMa generic domain model:

Element	Description
Client	Abstract class, representing a person plus corresponding contact information.
Contact	Contact information that will be used for contacting the client instances during campaign execution.
Next Action	Generic class describing campaign activities. Central to the concept of campaign process control and business rule execution

Figure 3.28: Elements of MaMa generic domain model

8.1.2 Example of a Campaign-Specific Domain Model

Specific campaign models always contain a (physical) copy of the complete core domain. The abstract **Client** class always needs to be subclassed and might be 1:n associated with additional classes. This is shown in the following diagram:

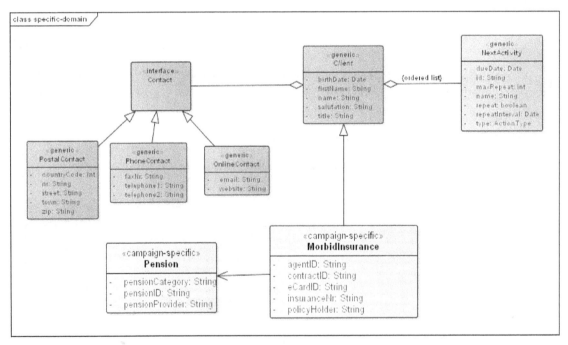

Figure 3.29: Specific Domain Model (for a hypothetical insurance campaign)

8.1.3 Generator Details

The following are the details of the specific domain model for MaMa deployment:

- MaMa uses **OpenArchitectureWare** to generate the complete persistence code.

- Generation relies on the open source Hibernate O/R mapping and persistence framework.

- The generator generated the elements, that is, the **Data Definition Language** (**DDL**) code to create the database, schema, tables, and indices, Hibernate mapping files, campaign-specific implementations of findClientByXY, findNextActivity, and similar methods, and a number of campaign- and configuration-specific methods for reporting and monitoring.

- *m:n* associations are not supported.

- We cannot modify data structures when the campaigns are already active.

Due to nondisclosure agreements with InDAC, we cannot show the example source code for the persistence concept.

Alternatives

- Initially, MaMa started with the AndroMDA code generation framework, but that open source project lost popularity, could not deliver the required support, and ceased working with newer Maven releases. Therefore, MaMa switched to OAW.

- MaMa uses the commercial MagicDraw UML (in version 9.0) modeling tool, which can, in principle, generate code based on models. However, it hasn't proved to be too inflexible for the desired Hibernate integration. The contracting entity (InDAC) refused to upgrade to newer versions or alternative tools.

8.2 CSV Import/Export

- TODO: Describe (some) details of the CSV configuration DSL
- TODO: Describe (customized) the Eclipse editor for these DSLs

8.3 Configurable File Filters

As explained in the runtime scenario *import raw*, every file that's read during an import from an external source needs to be transformed via configurable filters. We often have two kinds of filters: encryption and compression.

The names and required parameter settings for every filter are managed as part of the activity configuration within a campaign.

Encryption Filters

Encryption filters are compliant with the **Java Cryptography Architecture** (**JCA** – https://docs.oracle.com/javase/8/docs/technotes/guides/security/crypto/CryptoSpec.html) interfaces.

We urge mandators and partners to use crypto providers from the **BouncyCastle** (https://www.bouncycastle.org/java.html) portfolio. Encryption and decryption filters need credentials or certificates as part of their configuration.

> **Note**
>
> Due to the sensitive nature of the data that was handled by the original MaMa system, the owner required strict nondisclosure in that aspect. Therefore, we are not allowed to go into any details regarding security.

Compression Filter

MaMa supports only lossless compression algorithms. Compression can be configured to be either **DEFLATE** (as used in .zip or .gzip) or varieties of *Lempel-Ziv* compression. Compression filters have no parameters.

8.4 Rule Engine for Process and Flow Control

This section will focus on the set of rules that need to be followed for the process and workflow of MaMa deployment:

8.4.2 Drools as a Rule Engine

MaMa uses the open source rule engine Drools (www.drools.org) for the definition, implementation, and execution of business rules. Rules are defined as text files, which are interpreted at runtime by the rule engine. This enables the modification and maintenance of rules without recompilation and redeployment of the whole system.

On the other hand, faulty rules can seriously hamper an active campaign – therefore, the modification of business rules should always be thoroughly tested!

Rules always have a simple "when **<A>** then **<B>**" format, where **<A>** and **<B>** are Java expressions.

You can find a complete reference and many examples of the rule language in Drool's documentation (http://www.drools.org/learn/documentation.html).

III.9 Architecture Decisions

Following are the architectural decisions thaat are considered for MaMa:

* No commercial CRM tool:

  Do not use any of the commercial CRM tools as a foundation for MaMa. The main reason for this was the incredible amount of flexibility that was required to quickly set up campaigns. This decision proved to be correct, as several early competitors (who operated on slightly customized standard CRM tools) failed to enter the market MaMa operated in.

* JBoss Drools for rule processing:

  Use JBoss Drools as a rule processing engine. We evaluated Python (Jython) as an alternative, but that proved to be incredibly slow for our kind of processing.

* No ETL tool for data import:

  Do not use an ETL tool for importing data. The contractor, InDAC, refused to consider the license fee of commercial ETL tools. Therefore, the development team had no chance to even evaluate these tools as data import solutions.

III.10 Quality Scenarios

The following are the different types of quality scenarios that need to be taken care of:

Flexibility Scenarios

The following table depicts the flexibility scenarios that need to be considered for maintaining quality standards:

ID	Scenario
F1	New CSV import format shall be configurable at CCT within 2 hours.
F2	New fix-field import format shall be configurable at CCT within 2 hours.
F3	New XML based import format shall be configurable at CCT within 2 hours.
F4	New CSV export format shall be configurable at CCT within 2 hours.
F5	New fix-field export format shall be configurable at CCT within 2 hours.
F6	New XML based export format shall be configurable at CCT within 2 hours.

Figure 3.30: Flexibility scenarios

CCT: *Campaign configuration time*

In all cases, we require documentation of the desired format, plus a minimum of 10 different test data records.

Runtime Performance Scenarios

The following table depicts the runtime performance scenarios:

ID	Scenario
P1	Import and fully process 250.000 scanned documents (including images) within 24hrs. That's an average processing rate of approximately 3 complete documents per second. Import format will be a combination of csv file plus images as single files.
P2	Import and fully process 100.000 records of csv file within 30 minutes

Figure 3.31: Runtime performance scenarios

Security Scenarios

The following are the security scenarios to be considered:

ID	Scenario
S1	Client and campaign data from one mandator shall never be accessible for another mandator. III - Mass Market Customer Relationship Management 94
S2	MaMa is required to preserve all incoming data from mandators and partners for the appropriate timeframe (usually 90-180 days after the end of a campaign). Such archived data (e.g. files or messages) needs to be made completely accessible for an auditor or inspection within 90 minutes at most.
S3	In case campaigns involve financial data of clients (e.g. credit card, bank account or similar information), these have to be processed and managed compliant to PCIDSS[45] regulations.

Figure 3.32: Security Scenarios

III.11 Risks

Following are the risks that influence the architectural decisions:

- The **Receiver** component suffers from overly complicated source code that's created by a number of developers without consent. Most production bugs result from this part of MaMa-CRM.

- The runtime flexibility of import/export configurations and campaign processes might lead to incorrect and undetected behavior at runtime as there are no configuration checks. Mischievous administrators can misconfigure any MaMa-CRM instance at any time.

- Configuration settings are not archived and therefore might get lost (so there might be no fallback to the last working configuration in case of trouble).

- CoMcS is an overly trivial and resource-wasting synchronization mechanism and should be replaced with a decent async/event-based system as soon as possible.

III.12 Glossary

The following table defines the important terms used through the chapter.

Term	Definition
Activity	Process step of campaign. For MaMa-CRM: either inbound, outbound or internal.
Activity, internal	Scheduled data maintenance activities, i.e. removing some data 90 days after its last usage. In Germany, data security law requires some kinds of data to be deleted after certain intervals.
Activity, inbound	Read data (i.e. files) delivered by either a ->partner or ->mandator.
Activity, outbound	Send data to either a partner or mandator.
Branch office	Business organization directly associated with mandator, serves a subset of one mandators' consumers.
Campaign	Coordinated set of activities, initiated by a ->mandator towards a potentially large number of >clients. MaMaCRM campaigns usually aim at acquiring certain kinds of data, like passport photographs, social security numbers, signatures etc.
CID	Common Insurance ID, 10-digit number to uniqely identify an health insured person in Germany. Created by a central agency.
Client	aka: Consumer. Single person or company with a business relationship to mandator. The end user of the services or products provided by the mandator.
CSV	Comma Separated Value
End user	Synonym for consumer.
InDAC	Contractee of MaMa-CRM, the data-center that initiated and payed for its development. Provides CRM campaign services for several mandators.
Instance	MaMa-CRM is a family of systems, where a single instance is configured and operated for exactly one mandator and one or more campaigns.
Mandator	Organization responsible for a campaign. Conducts business in a mass-market domain like insurance, telecommunication, retail or energy.
Partner	Category name for service providers: Organization or enterprise providing services for MaMa, like printing, scanning, phone and call-center, mail delivery, and so forth.
PCIDSS	Payment Card Industry Data Security Standard[46], a collection of proprietary standards for secure handling and managemant of credit card related data.
RSN	Request sequence number, 0-padded 8-digit string containing the sequence number of CID requests.

Figure 3.33: Glossary terms

4

IV - biking2

By **Michael Simons**

biking2 or "Michis milage" is primarily a web-based application for tracking biking-related activities. It allows the user to track their covered milage, collect GPS tracks of routes and convert them into different formats, track their location, and publish pictures of bike tours.

The secondary goal of this application is to experiment with various technologies; for example, Spring Boot on the server side and AngularJS, JavaFX, and others on the client side.

biking2 has been around since 2009 and in its current Java-based form since 2014. With the production fulfilling its primary goal of releasing architecture for biking-related activities, it's been in production ever since.

The project is published under the Apache License on GitHub (https://github.com/ michael-simons/biking2), and you can use it however you like. Though I've been blogging regularly about this pet project, the documentation (in its current form) was created after I met Dr. Gernot and Peter at an awesome workshop in Munich.

IV.1 Introduction and Requirements

In this section, we will be looking at biking2 in depth and will study its requirements.

1.1 Requirements Overview

What is biking2?

The main purpose of biking2 is to keep track of bicycles and their milage, as well as converting **Garmin** files (https://en.wikipedia.org/wiki/Training_Center_XML) into standard files (https://en.wikipedia.org/wiki/GPS_Exchange_Format) and storing them in an accessible way.

In addition, biking2 is used to study and evaluate technology, patterns, and frameworks. The functional requirements are simple enough to leave enough room for us to concentrate on quality goals.

Main features

The following are the distinct features of biking2:

- It stores bikes and their milage
- It converts **tcx** files into **GPX** files and provides them in a library of tracks
- It visualizes those tracks on a map and provides a way to embed them in other web pages
- It visualizes biking activities with images
- It offers optional, near-real-time tracking of a biker

The application can only handle one user with write permissions. Most bike aficionados have problems understanding the question "why more than one bike?" As such, the system should be able to keep track of between 2 and 10 bikes for one user and store the total milage per bike and per month. All milage per month, milage per year, and other metrics should be derived from this running total so that the user only needs to look at their odometer and enter the value.

The application should store an "unlimited" number of tracks.

The images should be collected from (https://dailyfratze.de). The source contains images that are tagged with **Radtour**. In addition, the user should be able to provide an "unlimited" number of "gallery pictures," along with a date and a short description.

1.2 Quality Goals

The following are the quality goals that need to be considered:

- **Understandability**: The functional requirements are simple enough to allow a simple, understandable solution that lets us focus on learning about new Java 8 features, Spring Boot, and AngularJS.

- **Efficiency**: Collecting milage data should be a no-brainer; that is, reading the milage from an odometer and entering it.

- **Interoperability**: The application should provide a simple API that allows access to new clients.

- **Attractiveness**: Collected milage metrics should be presented in easy-to-grasp charts.

- **Testability**: The architecture should allow us to easily test the main building blocks.

1.3 Stakeholders

The following list explains the most important personas for this application:

- **Developers**: Developers who want to learn about developing modern applications with Spring Boot and various frontends, which should use Java 8 in the backend.

- **Bikers**: Bike aficionados who are looking for a non-Excel, self-hosted solution to keep track of their bikes and milage.

- **Software Architects**: Who are looking for an **arc42** example to get ideas for their daily work.

- **Michael Simons**: Improving his skills; wants to blog about Spring Boot; looking for a topic he can eventually hold a talk about; needed a project to try out new Java 8 features.

IV.2 Architecture Constraints

The constraints of this project are reflected in the final solution. This section explains them and, if applicable, their motivation.

2.1 Technical Constraints

The following table lists the various technical constraints of biking2:

	Constraint	Background and / or motivation
TC1	Software and programming constraints Implementation in Java	The application should be part of a Java 8 and Spring Boot show case. The interface (i.e. the api) should be language and framework gnostic, however. It should be possible that clients can be implemented using various frameworks and languages.
TC2	Third party software must be available under an compatible open source license and installable via a package manager	The interested developer or architect should be able to check out the sources, compile and run the application without problems compiling or installing dependencies. All external dependencies should be available via the package manager of the operation system or at least through an installer.
TC3	Operating System Constraints OS independent development	The application should be compilable on all 3 mayor operation systems (Mac OS X, Linux and Windows)
TC4	Deployable to a Linux server	The application should be deployable through standard means on a Linux based server
TC5	Hardware Constraints Memory friendly	Memory can be limited (due to availability on a shared host or deployment to cloud based host). If deployed to a cloud based solution, every megabyte of memory costs.

Figure 4.1: Technical constraints

2.2 Organizational Constraints

The following table lists the organizational constraints of biking2:

	Constraint	Background and / or motivation
OC1	Team	Michael Simons
OC2	Time schedule	Start in early 2014 with Spring Boot beta based prototypes running on Java 8 early access builds, first "release" version March 2014 together with the initial release of Java 8. Upgrade to a final Spring Boot release when they are available.
OC3	IDE independent project setup	No need to continue the editor and IDE wars. The project must be compilable on the command line via standard build tools. Due to OC2 there is only one IDE supporting Java 8 features out of the box: NetBeans 8 beta and release candidates.
OC4	Configuration and version control / management	Private git repository with a complete commit history and a public master branch pushed to GitHub and linked a project blog.
OC5	Testing	Use JUnit to prove functional correctness and integration tests and JaCoCo to ensure a high test coverage (at least 90%).
OC6	Published under an Open Source license	The source, including documentation, should be published as Open Source under the Apache 2 License

Figure 4.2: Organizational constraints

2.3 Conventions

The following table lists the various conventions followed:

	Conventions	Background and / or motivation
C1	Architecture documentation	Structure based on the english arc42-Template in version 6.5
C2	Coding conventions	The project uses the Code Conventions for the Java TM Programming Language[51]. The conventions are enforced through Checkstyle.
C3	Language	English. The project and the corresponding blog targets an international audience, so English should be used throughout the whole project.

Figure 4.3: Conventions used

The following naming conventions are used throughout the project:

- All Java types must be located in packages that start with **ac.simons** .

```
MATCH
(project:Maven:Project)-[:CREATES]->(:Artifact)-(:CONTAINS)->(type:Type)
WHERE
NOT type.fqn starts with 'ac.simons'
RETURN
project as Project, collect(type) as TypeWithWrongName
```

- All Java types must be located in packages that contains the **artifactld** of the Maven Project.

```
MATCH
(project:Maven:Project)-(:CREATES)->(:Artifact)-(:CONTAINS)->(type:Type)
WHERE
NOT type.fqn contains project.artifactld
RETURN
project as Project, collect(type) as TypeWithWrongName
```

- All Java types annotated as @Entity must have a name that ends with the suffix **Entity**.

```
MATCH
(t:Jpa:Entity)
WHERE
NOT t.name ends with "Entity"
RETURN
t as Entity
```

- All Java types that represent a repository must have a name that ends with the suffix **Repository**.

```
MATCH
(t:Repository)
WHERE t:Java
AND NOT t.name ends with "Repository" RETURN
t as Repository
```

IV.3 System Scope and Context

This section describes the environment and context of biking2: who uses the system and the other systems that biking2 depends on?

3.1 Business Context

The following figure depicts the business context setup for biking2:

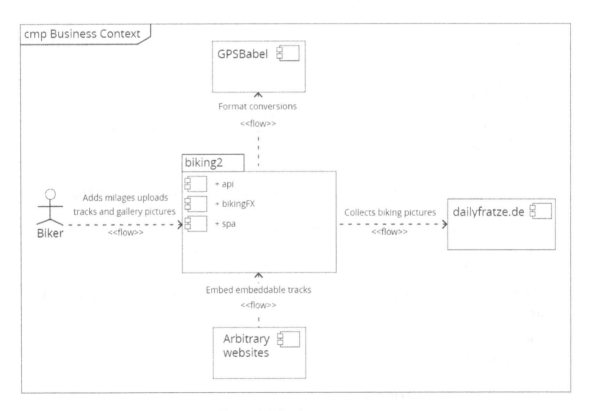

Figure 4.4: Business context

The following are the various components of the business context setup:

Biker

A passionate biker uses biking2 to manage their bikes, milage, tracks, and visual memories (that is, images) that they took on tours. They also want to embed their tracks as interactive maps on other websites.

Daily Fratze

Daily Fratze (https://dailyfratze.de) provides a list of images tagged with certain topics. biking2 should collect all the images for a given user tagged with "`Theme/Radtour`".

GPSBabel

GPSBabel is a command-line utility for manipulating GPS-related files in various ways. biking2 uses it to convert TCX files into GPX files. The heavy lifting is done by GPSBabel and the resulting file will be managed by biking2.

Arbitrary Websites

The user may want to embed (or brag about) tracks on arbitrary websites. They'll only want to paste a link to a track on a website that supports embedded content to embed a map with the given track.

3.2 Technical Context

The technical context setup is depicted in the following figure:

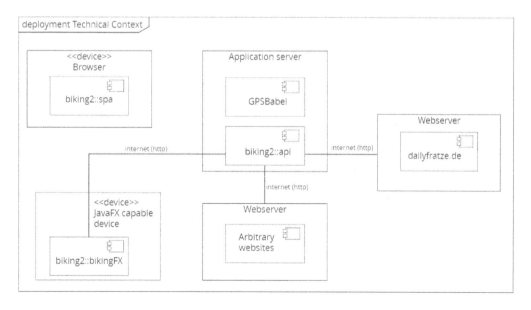

Figure 4.5: Technical context

biking2 is broken down into two main components: the backed and the frontend.

Backend (biking2::api)

The API runs on a supported application server using either an embedded container or an external container. It communicates via operating system processes with GPSBabel on the same server.

The connection to Daily Fratze is an HTTP-based RSS feed. The feed is paginated and provides all images with a given tag, but older images may not be available if the owner decides to add a digital expiry date.

Furthermore, biking2 provides an oEmbed (https://oembed.com) interface for all the tracks that are stored on the system. Arbitrary websites that support that protocol can request embeddable content over HTTP with only a link to the track without working on the track or map APIs themselves.

Frontend (biking2::spa and biking2::bikingFX)

The frontend is implemented with two different components, and the **biking2::spa** `Single-Page Application` (SPA) is part of this package. The SPA runs in any modern web browser and communicates with the API via HTTP.

The following table lists the various channels used by the different business interfaces:

Business interface	channel
Format conversions	System processes, command line interface
Collection of biking pictures	RSS feed over Internet (http)
Embeddable content	oEmbed format over Internet (http)
API for business functions	Internet (http)

Figure 4.6: List of business interfaces

IV.4 Solution Strategy

At the core of biking2 is a simple yet powerful domain model based on a few entities, of which a "Bike" and its "Milage" are the most important.

Although data-centric, the application refrains from using too much SQL to create reports, summaries, and so on, but tries to achieve that with new Java 8 features related to streams, lambdas, and map/reduce functions.

Building the application with Spring Boot is an obvious choice as one of the main quality goals is learning about it. Furthermore, using Spring Boot as a "framework" for Spring Framework allows us to concentrate on the business logic. On the one hand, there is no need to understand a complex XML configuration, while on the other, all of the building blocks are still put together using dependency injection.

Regarding dependency injection and testability, all injection should be done via constructor injection; setter injection is only allowed when there's no other technical way of completing the task at hand. This way, only units that are under test can be correctly instantiated; otherwise, we may forget about collaborators. Think of it this way: 20 injected attributes may not hurt, but a constructor with 20 parameters will. This hopefully prevents centralized "God classes" that control pretty much every other aspect of the application.

Spring Boot applications can be packaged as single `fat jar` files. Since Spring Boot 1.3, these files contain a startup script and can be directly linked to **`/etc/init.d`** on a standard Linux system that serves TC4.

Interoperability can be achieved by using JSON over a simple HTTP protocol for the main API. Security is not the main focus of this application. It should be secure enough to prevent others from tampering with the data, and so confidentiality is not a main concern (passwords can be transmitted in plain text over HTTP).

The internal single-page application (SPA) will be implemented using AngularJS. The deployable artifact will contain this application, so there is no need to host a second web server for the static files.

For real-time tracking, the MQTT protocol will be used, which is part of Apache ActiveMQ and is supported out of the box by Spring messaging.

Graphing should not be implemented here; instead, the **Highcharts** (https://www. highcharts.com) library should be used. The configuration for all charts should be computed on the server side.

IV.5 Building Blocks-Level 1

The application that's packaged as **biking2.jar** contains two of three main parts (the **api** and the **spa**), as shown in the business context:

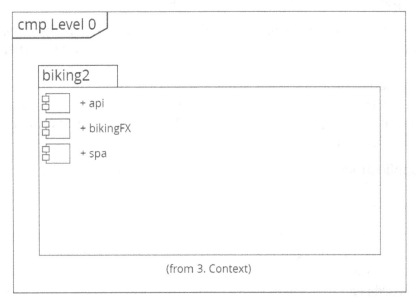

Figure 4.7: Level 0 building blocks

Let's have a closer look at the API. For details regarding the structure of an AngularJS 1.2.x application, have a look at their developer's guide (https://code.angularjs. org/1.2.28/docs/guide).

Note

To comply with the Java coding style guidelines, the"**bikingPictures**" and "**galleryPictures**" modules reside in the "**bikingpictures**" and "**gallerypictures**" Java packages.

5.1 Whitebox biking2::api

The following diagram shows the main building blocks of the system and their interdependencies:

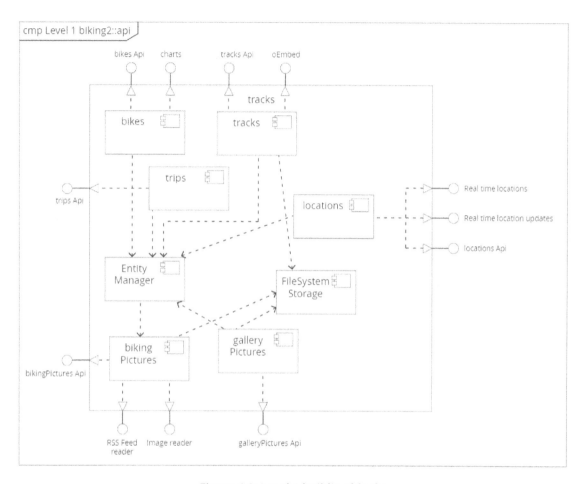

Figure 4.8: Level 1 building blocks

I used functional decomposition to separate responsibilities. The single parts of the API are all encapsulated in their own components, represented as Java packages.

All of the components depend on a standard JPA **EntityManager** and some local file storage. I won't go into detail about those black boxes.

Contained Blackboxes

Blackbox	Purpose
bikes (Blackbox)	Managing bikes, adding monthly milages, computing statistics and generating charts.
tracks (Blackbox)	Uploading tracks (TCX files), converting to GPX, providing an oEmbed interface.
trips (Blackbox)	Managing assorted trips.
locations (Blackbox)	MQTT and STOMP interface for creating new locations and providing them in real time on websockets via stomp.
bikingPictures (Blackbox)	Reading biking pictures from an RSS feed provided by Daily Fratze and providing an API to them.
galleryPictures (Blackbox)	Uploading and managing arbitrary pictures

Figure 4.9: Contained blackboxes

All the blackboxes above should correspond to Java packages. Those packages should have no dependencies to other packages outside themselves but for the support or shared package:

- Top level packages should conform to the main building blocks.

```
MATCH (a:Main:Artifact)
MATCH (a) -[:CONTAINS]-> (p1:Package) -[:DEPENDS_ON]-> (p2:Package)
<-[:CONTAINS]- (a) WHERE not p1:Config
and not (p1) -[:CONTAINS]-> (p2)
and not p2:Support
and not p1.fqn = 'ac.simons.biking2.summary'
RETURN p1, p2
```

Additional configuration apart from properties lives in the **config** package:

- Returns the **config** package.

```
MATCH (p:Package)
WHERE p.fqn in Uac.simons.biking2.configi SET p:Package:Config
return p
```

The **support** package contains technical infrastructure classes while the shared package contains application wide messages. Those packages are used as supporting packages:

- Returns **support** and **shared** packages.

```
MATCH (p:Package)
WHERE p.fqn in ['ac.simons.biking2.shared', 'ac.simons.biking2.support']
SET p:Package:Support
return p
```

Interfaces

Interface	Description
bikes Api	REST api containing methods for reading, adding and decommissioning bikes and for adding milages to single bikes.
charts	Methods for retrieving statistics as fully setup chart definitions.
tracks Api	REST api for uploading and reading TCX files.
trips Api	REST api for adding new trips.
oEmbed	HTTP based oEmbed interface, generating URLs with embeddable content. Real time locations, WebSocket / STOMP based interface on which new locations are published.
Real time location updates	MQTT interface to which MQTT compatible systems like OwnTracks[56] can offer location updates.
RSS feed reader	Needs an Daily Fratze OAuth token for accessing a RSS feed containing biking pictures which are than grabbed from Daily Fratze.
galleryPictures Api	REST api for uploading and reading arbitrary image files (pictures related to biking).

Figure 4.10: Interfaces

5.1.1 bikes (Blackbox)

Intent/responsibility: bikes provides the external API for reading, creating, and manipulating bikes and their milage, as well as computing statistics and generating charts.

The following table includes a list of different interfaces:

Interface	Description
REST interface /api/bikes/*	Contains all methods for manipulating bikes and their milages.
REST interface /api/charts/*	Contains all methods for generating charts.

Figure 4.11: Interface for REST

Files

The bikes module and all of its dependencies are contained inside a Java package called `ac.simons.biking2.bikes`.

5.1.2 tracks (Blackbox)

Intent/responsibility: tracks manages file uploads (TCX files), converts them into GPX files, and computes their surrounding rectangle (envelope) using GPSBabel. It also provides the oEmbed interface, which resolves URLS to embeddable tracks.

Files

Interface	Description
REST interface /api/tracks/*	Contains all methods for manipulating tracks.
/api/oembed	Resolve track URLs to embeddable tracks (content).
/tracks/*	Embeddable track content.

Figure 4.12: Interfaces for files

The **tracks** module and all of its dependencies are contained inside a Java package called `ac.simons.biking2.tracks`.

5.1.3 trips (Blackbox)

Intent/responsibility: trips manages distances that have been covered on single days without relationships to bikes:

Interface	Description
REST interface /api/trips/*	Contains all methods for manipulating trips.

Figure 4.13: Trips

Files

The **trips** module and all of its dependencies are contained inside a Java package called `ac.simons.biking2.trips`.

5.1.4 locations (Blackbox)

locations stores locations with timestamps in near real time and provides access to locations for the last 30 minutes.

Interfaces

The following table describes the various interfaces used:

Interface	Description
REST interface /api/locations/*	For retrieving all locations in the last 30 minutes.
WebSocket / STOMP topic /topic/currentLocation	Interface for getting notifcation on new locations.
MQTT interface	Listens for new locations coming in via MQTT in OwnTracks format[57]

Figure 4.14: Interfaces

> **Note**
>
> For more information on OwnTracks, please refer to: https://owntracks.org/booklet/tech/json/

Files

The **locations** module and all of its dependencies are contained inside a Java package called **ac.simons.biking2.tracker**. The module is configured through the **ac.simons.biking2.config.TrackerConfig** class.

5.1.5 bikingPictures (Blackbox)

Intent/responsibility: **bikingPictures** is used to regularly check an RSS feed from Daily Fratze while collecting new images and storing them locally. It also provides an API for getting all the collected images.

Interfaces

Interface	Description
RSS Feed reader	Provides access to the Daily Fratze RSS Feed.
Image reader	Provides access to images hosted on Daily Fratze.
REST interface /api/bikingPictures/*	Contains all methods for accessing biking pictures

Figure 4.15: Interfaces

Files

The **bikingPictures** module and all of its dependencies are contained inside a Java package called **ac.simons.biking2.bikingpictures**.

5.1.6 galleryPictures (Blackbox)

Intent/responsibility: **galleryPictures** manages file uploads (images). It stores them locally and provides an RSS interface for getting metadata and image data.

Interfaces

Interface	Description
REST interface /api/galleryPictures/*	Contains all methods for adding and reading arbitrary pictures.

Figure 4.16: Interfaces

Files

The **galleryPictures** module and all of its dependencies are contained inside a Java package called **ac.simons.biking2.gallerypictures**.

5.2 Building Blocks – Level 2

5.2.1 bikes (Whitebox)

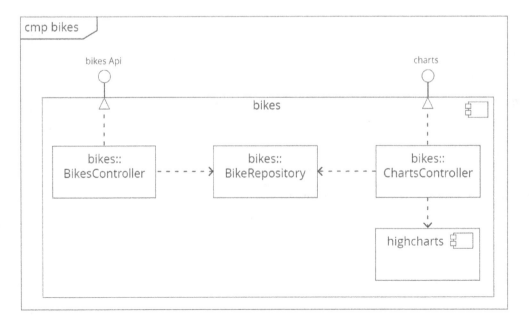

Figure 4.17: Building block – bikes

BikeRepository is a Spring Data JPA-based repository for `BikeEntities`. **BikeController** and **ChartsController** access it to retrieve and store instances of `BikeEntity` and provide external interfaces.

Contained Blackboxes

Blackbox	Purpose
highcharts	Contains logic for generating configurations and definitions for Highcharts[58] on the server side.

Figure 4.18: Blackboxes

5.2.2 tracks (Whitebox)

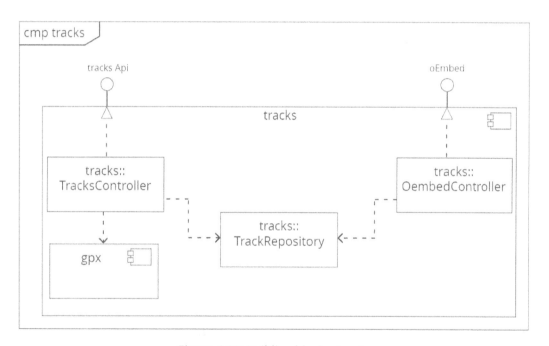

Figure 4.19: Building block – tracks

TrackRepository is a Spring Data JPA-based repository for `TrackEntities`. **TracksController** and **OembedController** access it to retrieve and store instances of `TrackEntity` and provide external interfaces.

Contained Blackboxes

Blackbox	Purpose
gpx	Generated JAXB classes for parsing GPX files. Used by the TracksController to retrieve the surrounding rectangle (envelope) for new tracks.

Figure 4.20: Blackbox

5.2.3 trips (Whitebox)

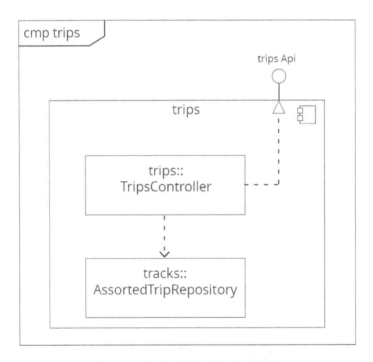

Figure 4.21: Building block – trips

AssortedTripRepository is a Spring Data JPA-based repository for
AssortedTripEntities. **TripsController** accesses it to retrieve and store instances of
`TrackEntity` and provide external interfaces.

5.2.4 locations (Whitebox)

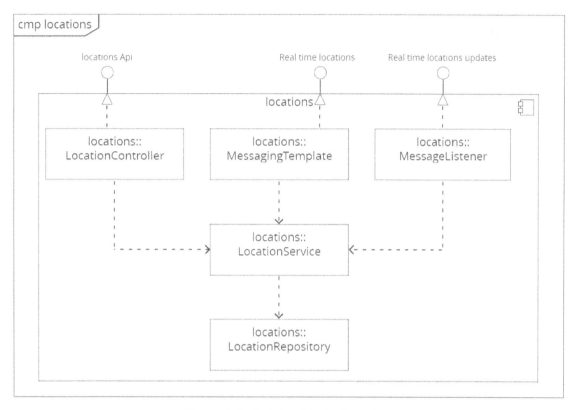

Figure 4.22: Building block – locations

Locations are stored and read via a Spring Data JPA-based repository named **LocationRepository**. This repository is only accessed through **LocationService**. This provides real-time updates for connected clients through `SimpMessagingTemplate`, and **LocationController** uses the service to provide access to all the locations that have been created within the last 30 minutes.

New locations are created by the service either through a REST interface in the form of **LocationController** or via a **MessageListener** on an MQTT channel.

5.2.5 bikingPictures (Whitebox)

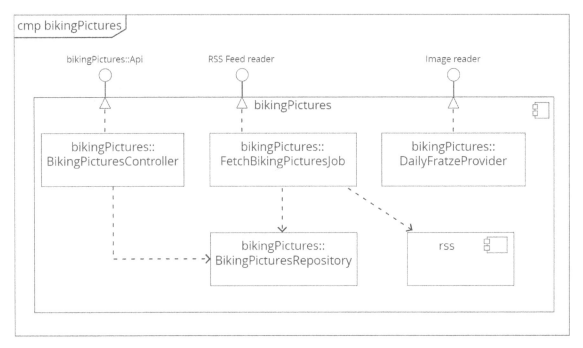

Figure 4.23: Building block – bikingPictures

A Spring Data JPA repository named **BikingPicturesRepository** is used to gain access to `BikingPictureEntities`. The external REST API for reading pictures is implemented with **BikingPicturesController**. The RSS feed is read from **FetchBikingPicturesJob** by using a `JAXBContext` called "**rss**." The URLs to the image files, which are protected by various means, are provided to the job via **DailyFratzeProvider**.

Contained Blackboxes

Blackbox	Purpose
rss	Generated JAXB classes for parsing RSS feeds. Used by the FetchBikingPicturesJob to read the contents of an RSS feed.

Figure 4.24: Blackbox

5.2.6 galleryPictures (Whitebox)

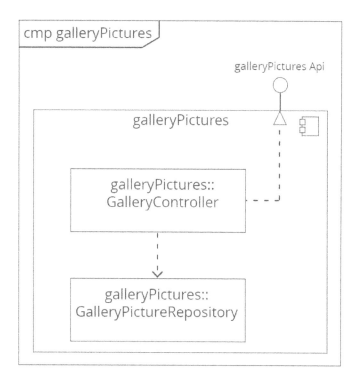

Figure 4.25: Building block – galleryPictures

GalleryPictureRepository is a Spring Data JPA-based repository for `GalleryPictureEntity`.

GalleryController accesses it to retrieve and store instances of `GalleryPictureEntity` and provide external interfaces.

IV.6 Runtime View

User interaction with biking2 and error handling is pretty basic. I picked up two use cases where an actual runtime view is interesting.

Creating New Tracks

The following figure depicts the process of creating new tracks:

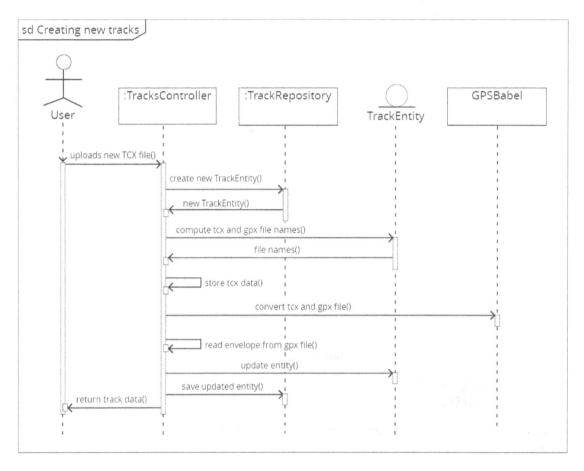

Figure 4.26 – Creating new tracks

Fetching Biking Pictures from Daily Fratze

The following figure shows how biking pictures are fetched from the Daily Fratze:

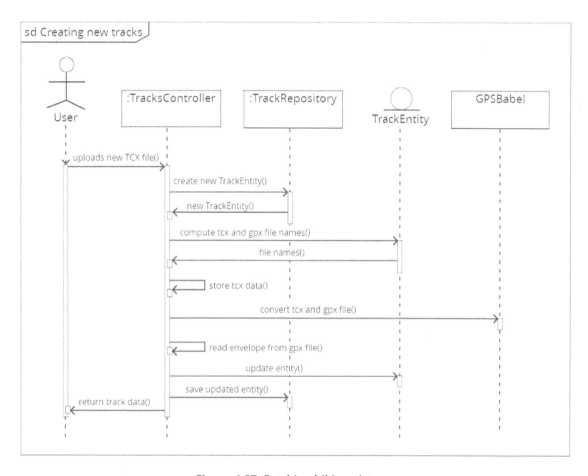

Figure 4.27: Fetching biking pictures

IV.7 Deployment View

The following figure shows you the deployment view of the biking application:

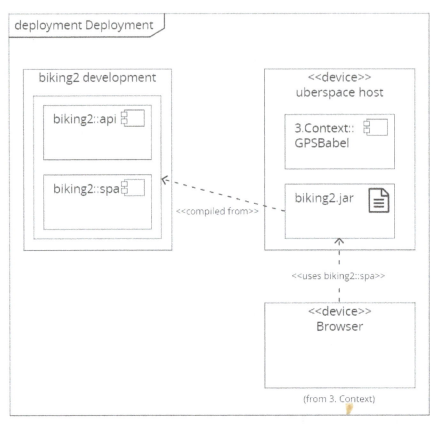

Figure 4.28: Deployment view

The following table describes the various nodes used in the deployment of the application:

Node / artifact	Description
biking2 development	Where biking2 development takes place, standard computer with JDK 8, Maven and GPSBabel installed.
uberspace host	A host on Uberspace[59] where biking2.jar runs inside a Server JRE[60] with restricted memory usage.
biking2.jar	A "fat jar" containing all Java dependencies and a loader so that the Jar is runnable either as jar file or as a service script (on Linux hosts).
Browser	A recent browser to access the AngularJS biking2 single page application. All major browsers (Chrome, Firefox, Safari, IE / Edge) should work.

Figure 4.29: Nodes

IV.8 Technical and Crosscutting Concepts

This section focusses on the technical concepts and other important concepts involved in the application.

Domain Models

biking2 is a data-centric application; therefore, everything is based around the following Entity Relationship Diagram (ERD):

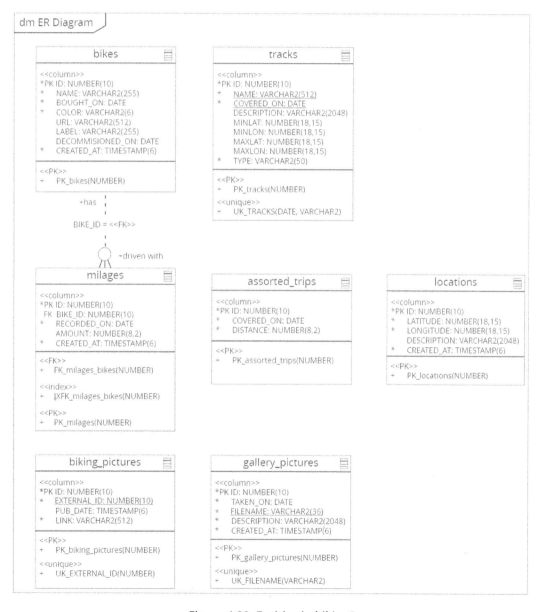

Figure 4.30: Entities in biking2

These entities are manifested as tables.

Tables

Name	Description
bikes	Stores the bikes. Contains dates when the bike was bought and decomissioned, an optional link, color for the charts and also an auditing column when a row was created.
milages	Stores milages for a bike (when and how much).
tracks	Stores GPS tracks recorded and uploaded with an optional description. For each day the track names must be unique. The columns minlat, minlon, maxlat and maxlon store the encapsulating rectangle for the track. The type column is constrainted to "biking" and "running".
assorted_trips	Stores a date and a distance on that day. Multiple distances per day are allowed.
locations	Stores arbitrary locations (latitude and longitude based) for given timestamp with an optional description.
biking_pictures	Stores pictures collected from Daily Fratze together with their original date of publication, their unique external id and a link to the page the picture originaly appeared.
gallery_pictures	Stores all pictures uploaded by the user with a description and the date the picture was taken. The filename column contains a single, computed filename without path information.

Figure 4.31: Tables

Those tables are mapped to the following domain model:

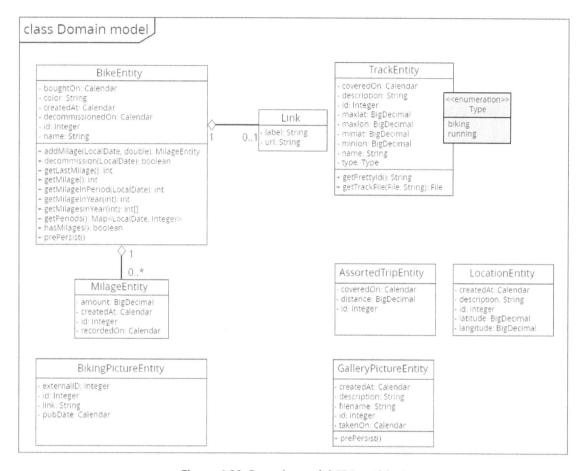

Figure 4.32: Domain model (JPA entities)

Domain Model

Name	Description
BikeEntity	A bike was bought on a given date and can be decommisioned. It has a color and an optional link to an arbitrary website. It may or may not have milages recorded. It has some important functions.
MilageEntity	A milage is part of a bike. For each bike one milage per month can be recored. The milage is the combination of it's recording date, the amount and the bike.
TrackEntity	The representation of tracks contents. The type is an enumeration. Notable public operations are getPrettyId (computes a "pretty" id based on the instances id) and getTrackFile (generates a reference to the GPS track file in the passed data storage directory).
BikingPictureEntity	For handling pictures collected from Daily Fratze. The BikingPictureEntity parses the image link on construction and retrieves the unique, external id.
GalleryPictureEntity	A bean for handling the pictures uploaded by the user. prePersist fills the createdAt attribute prior to inserting into the database.
AssortedTripEntity	This entity captures a distance which was covered on a certain date and can be used for keeping track of trips with bikes not stored in this application for example.
LocationEntity	Used in the tracker module for working with real time locations.

Figure 4.33: Domain model components

Important Business Methods Regarding BikeEntity

Name	Description
decommission	Decommissions a bike on a given date.
addMilage	Adds a new milage for a given date and returns it. The milage will only be added if the date is after the date the last milage was added and if the amount is greater than the last milage.
getPeriods	Gets all monthly periods in which milages havebeen recorded.
getMilage	Gets the total milage of this bike.
getLastMilage	Gets the last milage recorded. In most cases the same as getMilage.
getMilageInPeriod	Gets the milage in a given period.
getMilagesInYear	Gets all milages in a year as an array (of months).
getMilageInYear	Gets the total milage in a given year.

Figure 4.34: Business methods

Persistency

biking2 uses an H2 (https://www.h2database.com/html/main.html) database for storing relational data and the filesystem for binary image files and large ASCII files (especially all GPS files).

During development and production, the H2 database is retained and is not in-memory-based. The location of this file is configured through the `biking2.database-file` property and the default value during development is `./var/dev/db/biking-dev`, which is relative to the working directory of the VM.

All access to the database goes through JPA, which uses Hibernate as the provider. See the *Domain Models* for all the entities that are used in the application. The JPA Entity Manager isn't accessed directly – it can only be accessed through the facilities offered by Spring Data JPA; that is, through repositories. All the data that's stored as files is stored relative to `biking2.datastore-base-directory`, which defaults to `./var/dev`. Inside are three directories:

- `bikingPictures`: Contains all the pictures that were collected from Daily Fratze

- `galleryPictures`: Contains all the uploaded pictures

- `tracks`: Contains the uploaded GPS data and the results of converting TCX files into GPX files

User Interface

The default user interface for biking2 that's packaged within the final artifact is an SPA written in JavaScript using AngularJS, together with a default Bootstrap template.

To use the real-time location update interface, choose one of the many MQTT clients out there.

There is a second user interface written in Java, called bikingFX (https://info.michael-simons.eu/2014/10/22/getting-started-with-javafx-8-developing-a-rest-client-application-from-scratch/).

JavaScript and CSS Optimization

JavaScript and CSS dependencies are managed through Maven dependencies in the form of webjars (https://www.webjars.org) wherever possible, without the need for `brew`, `npm`, `bower`, and so on.

Furthermore, biking2 uses `wro4j` (https://alexo.github.io/wro4j/), along with a small Spring Boot Starter (https://github.com/michael-simons/wro4j-spring-boot-starter) to optimize JavaScript and CSS web resources.

Wro4j Configuration

wro4j provides a model like this:

```
<groups xmlns="http://www.isdc.ro/wro">
<!-- Dependencies for the full site -->
<group name="biking2">
<group-ref>osm</group-ref>

<css minimize="false">/webjars/bootstrap/@bootstrap.version@/css/b\
ootstrap.min.css</css>
<css>/css/stylesheet.css</css>

<js minimize="false">/webjars/jquery/@jquery.version@/jquery.min.j\
s</js>
<js minimize="false">/webjars/bootstrap/@bootstrap.version@/js/boo\
tstrap.min.js</js>
<js minimize="false">/webjars/momentjs/@momentjs.version@/min/mome\
nt-with-locales.min.js</js>
<js minimize="false">/webjars/angular-file-upload/@angular-file-up\
load.version@/angular-file-upload-html5-shim.min.js</js>
<js minimize="false">/webjars/angularjs/@angularjs.version@/angula\
r.min.js</js>
<js minimize="false">/webjars/angularjs/@angularjs.version@/angula\
r-route.min.js</js>
<js minimize="false">/webjars/angular-file-upload/@angular-file-up\
load.version@/angular-file-upload.min.js</js>
<js minimize="false">/webjars/angular-ui-bootstrap/@angular-ui-boo\
tstrap.version@/ui-bootstrap.min.js</js>
<js minimize="false">/webjars/angular-ui-bootstrap/@angular-ui-boo\
tstrap.version@/ui-bootstrap-tpls.min.js</js>
<js minimize="false">/webjars/highcharts/@highcharts.version@/high\
charts.js</js>
<js minimize="false">/webjars/highcharts/@highcharts.version@/high\
```

```
charts-more.js</js>
<js minimize="false">/webjars/sockjs-client/@sockjs-client.version\
@/sockjs.min.js</js>
<js minimize="false">/webjars/stomp-websocket/@stomp-websocket.ver\
sion@/stomp.min.js</js>
<js>/js/app.js</js>
<js>/js/controllers.js</js>
<js>/js/directives.js</js>
</group>
</groups>
```

This model file is filtered by the Maven build. Version placeholders will be replaced and all the resources that are in **webjars**, as well as inside the filesystem, will be available as **biking.css** and **biking.js** files, respectively.

How those files are optimized, minimized, or otherwise processed is up to wro4j's configuration, but minification can be turned off during development.

Transaction Processing

biking2 relies on Spring Boot to create all the necessary beans for handling local transactions within the JPA EntityManager. biking2 does not support distributed transactions.

Session Handling

biking2 only provides a stateless public API; there is no session handling.

Security

biking2 offers security for its API endpoints, but only via HTTP basic access authentication (https://cn.wikipedia.org/wiki/Basic_access_authentication). In the case of the MQTT module, it uses MQTT's default security model. Security can be increased by running the application behind an SSL proxy or configuring SSL support in the embedded Tomcat container. For the kind of data that's managed here, it's an agreed trade-off to keep the application simple. See the Safety section for more information.

Safety

No part of the system has life-endangering aspects.

Communication and Integration

biking2 uses an internal Apache ActiveMQ broker on the same VM as the application to provide STOMP channels and an MQTT transport. This broker is volatile, so messages are not persisted during application restarts.

Plausibility and Validity Checks

Data types and ranges are checked via **JSR-303**(https://beanvalidation.org/1.0/spec/) annotations on classes representing the Domain Models. Those classes are directly bound to external REST interfaces.

There are three important business checks:

1. Bikes that have been decommissioned cannot be modified (that is, they can have no new milage). Checked in **BikesController**.

2. For each month, only one milage can be added for a bike. Checked in **BikeEntity**.

3. A new milage must be greater than the last one. Also checked inside **BikeEntity**.

Exception/Error Handling

Errors handling inconsistent data (in regard to the data model's constraint) as well as validation failures are mapped to HTTP errors. These errors are handled by the frontend's controller code. Technical errors (hardware, database, and so on) are not handled and may lead to application failure or lost data.

Logging and Tracing

Spring Boot configures logging to standard out by default. The default configuration isn't changed in that regard, so all the framework logging (especially Spring and Hibernate) go to standard out in standard format and can be grabbed or ignored via OS-specific means.

All of the business components use the Simple Logging Facade for Java (SLF4J). The actual configuration of logging is configured through Spring Boot. No special implementation is included manually; instead, biking2 depends transitively on spring-boot-starter-logging.

The names of the logger correspond with the package names of the classes that instantiate loggers so that the modules are immediately recognizable in the logs.

Configurability

Spring Boot offers a plethora of configuration options. These are the main options for configuring Spring Boot and there are starters that are available: Common application properties (https://docs.spring.io/spring-boot/docs/current/reference/html/common-application-properties.html).

The default configuration is available in **src/main/resources/application.properties**.

During development, these properties are merged with **src/main/resources/application-dev.p**. Additional properties can be added through the system environment or through **application-*.properties** in the current JVM directory.

During tests, an additional **application-test.properties** can be used to add or overwrite additional properties or values.

The following are the biking2-specific properties:

Property	Default	Description
biking2.color-ofcumulative-graph	000000	Color of the cumulative line graph
biking2.dailyfratzeaccess-token	n/a	An OAuth access token for Daily Fratze
biking2.datastorebase-directory	${user.dir}/var/dev	Directory for storing files (tracks and images)
biking2.fetch-bikingpicture-cron	0 0 */8 * * *	A cron expression for configuring the FetchBikingPicturesJob
biking2.home.longitude	6.179489185520004	Longitude of thehome coordinate
biking2.home.latitude	50.75144902272457	Latitude of the home coordinate
biking2.connector.proxyName	n/a	The name of a proxy if biking2 runs behind one
biking2.connector.proxyPort	80	The port of a proxy if biking2 runs behind one
biking2.gpsBabel	/opt/local/bin/gpsbabel	Fully qualified path to the GPSBabel binary
biking2.scheduledthread-pool-size	10	Thread pool size for the job pool
biking2.tracker.host	localhost	The host on which the tracker (MQTT channel) should listen
biking2.tracker.stompPort	2307	STOMP port
biking2.tracker.mqttPort	4711	MQTT port
biking2.tracker.username	${security.user.name}	Username for the MQTT channel
biking2.tracker.password	${security.user.password}	Password for the MQTT channel
biking2.tracker.device	iPhone	Name of the OwnTracks device

Figure 4.35: biking2 properties

Internationalization

The only supported language is English. There is no hook for doing internationalization in the frontend and there are no plans for creating one.

Migration

biking2 replaced a Ruby application based on the Sinatra framework. Data was stored in a SQLite database that had been migrated by hand to the H2 database.

Testability

The project contains JUnit tests in the standard location of a Maven project. At the time of writing, those tests cover more than 95% of the code written. Tests must be executed during the build phase and should not be skipped.

Build Management

The application can be built with Maven without external dependencies outside of Maven. gpsbabel must be on the path to run all the tests, though.

IV.9 Architecture Decisions

We will now look into the various factors that will influence the architectural decisions to be made while building the application.

Using GPSBabel to Convert TCX into GPX Format

Problem

Popular JavaScript mapping frameworks allow us to include geometries from GPX data on maps. Most Garmin devices, however, record track data in TCX format, so I needed a way to convert TCX into GPX. Both formats are relatively simple and, especially in the case of GPX, are well-documented formats.

Constraints

- Conversion should handle TCX files with single tracks, laps, and additional points without any problems.

- The focus of this project has been on developing a modern application backend for an AngularJS SPA, not parsing GPX data.

Assumptions

- Using an external, non-Java-based tool makes it harder for people who just want to try out this application.

- Although well-documented, both file types can contain a variety of information (routes, tracks, waypoints, and so on), which makes them hard to parse.

Considered Alternatives

- Writing my own converter.

- Using an existing Swiss-Army knife for GPS data; that is, GPSBabel (https://www.gpsbabel.org). **GPSBabel** converts waypoints, tracks, and routes between popular GPS receivers such as Garmin or Magellan and mapping programs such as Google Earth or Basecamp. Literally hundreds of GPS receivers and programs are supported. It also has powerful manipulation tools for such data. These are used for filtering duplicates points or simplifying tracks, for example. It has been downloaded and used tens of millions of times since it was first created in 2001, so it's stable and trusted.

Decision

biking2 uses **GPSBabel** for the heavy lifting of GPS-related data. The project contains a README file stating that **GPSBabel** must be installed. **GPSBabel** can be installed on Windows with an installer and on most Linux systems through the official packet manager. For OS X, it is available via MacPorts or Homebrew.

Using Local File Storage for Image and Track Data

Problem

biking2 needs to store "large" objects; that is, image data (biking and gallery pictures) as well as track data.

Considered Alternatives

- Using cloud storage, such as S3
- Using the local filesystem

Decision

I opted for my local filesystem because I didn't want to put too much effort into evaluating cloud services. If biking2 is being run in a cloud-based setup, we have to create an abstraction over the local filesystem that's currently being used.

IV.10 Quality Scenarios

The following are the various quality scenarios that need to be taken care of while building the application.

10.1 Quality Tree

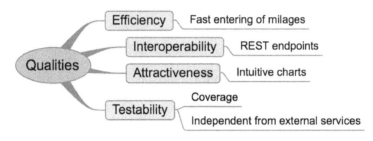

Figure 4.36: Quality tree

10.2 Evaluation Scenarios

Testability/Coverage

Using **JaCoCo** during development and the build process (https://info.michael-simons.eu/2014/05/22/jacoco-maven-and-netbeans-8-integration/) ensures that we get at least 95% code coverage.

Testability/Independent from External Services

The architecture should be designed in such a way that algorithms that depend on external services can be tested without having the external service available; that is, all the external dependencies should be mockable.

For example, `FetchBikingPicturesJob` needs a resource containing an RSS feed. Retrieving the resource and parsing it are at least two different tasks. Fetching the resource through a separate class, `DailyFratzeProvider`, makes testing the actual parsing independent from an HTTP connection and thus relatively simple.

IV.11 Risks

biking2 has been up and running for nearly 2 years now, and the architecture contains no known risks for my usage scenario.

There is a possibility that the H2 database could be damaged due to the unexpected shutdown of the VM (that is, OS or hardware failure). This risk is mitigated by regularly backing up the serialized database file:

IV.12 Glossary

Term	Synonym(s)	Description
AngularJS		AngularJS[1] is an open-source web application framework mainly maintained by Google and by a community of individual developers and corporations to address many of the challenges encountered in developing single-page applications.
Apache ActiveMQ		Apache ActiveMQ[2] is an open source message broker written in Java.
Apache License		The Apache License[3] is a permissive Open Source license, especially designed for free software.
Bootstrap		Bootstrap[4] is the most popular HTML, CSS, and JS framework for developing responsive, mobile first projects on the web.
Checkstyle		Checkstyle[5] is a development tool to help programmers write Java code that adheres to a coding standard. It automates the process of checking Java code to spare humans of this boring (but important) task. This makes it ideal for projects that want to enforce a coding standard.
Daily Fratze	df, DF, DailyFratze	An online community where users can upload a daily picture of themselves (a selfie, but the site did them before they where called selfies).
Fat Jar		A way of packaging Java applications into one single Jar file containing all dependencies, either repackaged or inside their original jars together with a special class loader.
Gallery picture		Pictures from tours provided manually by the hours in addition to the pictures collected automatically from Daily Fratze.
Garmin		Garmin[6] develops consumer, aviation, outdoor, fitness, and marine technologies for the Global Positioning System.
GPSBabel		GPSBabel[7] is a command line utility that converts waypoints, tracks, and routes between popular GPS receivers such as Garmin or Magellan and mapping programs like Google Earth or Basecamp.
GPX	GPS Exchange Format	GPX, or GPS Exchange Format, is an XML schema designed as a common GPS data format for software applications. It can be used to describe waypoints, tracks, and routes.
JaCoCo		JaCoCo[8] is a code coverage library which can be used very easily from within NetBeans.
JUnit		JUnit[9] is a simple framework to write repeatable tests. It is an instance of the xUnit architecture for unit testing frameworks.
MQTT	MQ Telemetry Transport	MQTT[10] is a publish-subscribe based "light weight" messaging protocol for use on top of the TCP/IP protocol.
NetBeans		NetBeans[11] is a free and open Source IDE that fits the pieces of modern development together.
OAuth		OAuth[12] is an open standard for authorization. OAuth provides client applications a 'secure delegated access' to server resources on behalf of a resource owner.
oEmbed		The oEmbed[13] protocol is a simple and lightweight format for allowing an embedded representation of an URL on third party sites.
RSS	Rich Site Summary, Really Simple Syndication	RSS[14] uses a family of standard web feed formats to publish frequently updated information: blog entries, news headlines, audio, video.
SLF4J	Simple Logging Facade for Java	The Simple Logging Facade for Java (SLF4J)[15] serves as a simple facade or abstraction for various logging frameworks (e.g. java.util.logging, logback, log4j) allowing the end user to plug in the desired logging framework at deployment time.
SPA	spa	Single Page Application
Spring Boot		Spring Boot[16] makes it easy to create stand-alone, production-grade Spring based Applications that you can "just run".
Spring Data JPA		Spring Data JPA[17], part of the larger Spring Data family, makes it easy to easily implement JPA based repositories.
STOMP	The Simple Text Oriented Messaging Protocol	STOMP[18] provides an interoperable wire format so that STOMP clients can communicate with any STOMP message broker to provide easy and widespread messaging interoperability among many languages, platforms and brokers.
TCX		Training Center XML (TCX) is a data exchange format introduced in 2007 as part of Garmin's Training Center product.

Figure 4.37: Glossary terms

5

V - DokChess

By **Stefan Zörner**

"Someday computers will make us all obsolete." - *Robert ("Bobby") Fisher, World Chess Champion 1972-1975, in 1975.*

This chapter describes the architecture of the chess program *DokChess*. I originally created it as an example for presentations and training on software architecture and design. Later on, I implemented it in Java and refined it for a German book on documenting software architectures (see http://www.swadok.de). The source code is available on GitHub and more information can be found at http://www.dokchess.de:

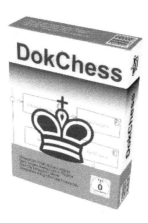

Figure 5.1: DokChess virtual product box

In the following architectural overview, you will learn about the important design decisions of DokChess. It shows the requirements that relate to the structure and design, basic solutions to problems, the structure of the software, and the interaction of key elements. The outline of the content follows the arc42 template.

The target audience of this architectural overview is primarily software architects seeking advice and examples on how to document architecture appropriately.

Software developers who plan to create a chess program of their own will learn some valuable tips and will learn about software architecture too.

V.1 Introduction and Requirements

This section introduces the task and outlines the objectives pursued by DokChess.

1.1 Requirements Overview

DokChess

The following are the distinct features of DokChess:

- DokChess is a fully functional chess engine.
- It serves both as an easily accessible and attractive case study of software architecture design, evaluation, and documentation.
- The understandable structure invites developers to experiment and to extend the engine.
- A high level of chess ability is not the goal. Nevertheless, DokChess manages to play games that casual chess players will enjoy.

Essential Features

Here are some of the essential features of DokChess:

- Complete compliance with the FIDE Laws of Chess
- Supports games against human opponents and other chess programs
- Masters fundamental chess tactics, such as fork and skewer
- Works with modern graphical chess frontends

1.2 Quality Goals

The following table describes the key quality objectives of DokChess. The order of the goals gives you a rough idea of their importance:

Quality Goal	Motivation/description
Accessible example (Analysability)	Since DokChess first of all serves as a case study for software architects and developers, they quickly get the idea of design and implementation.
Platform appealing to experiments (Changeability)	Alternative algorithms and strategies, such as the evaluation of a chess position, can be implemented and integrated into the solution easily.
Using existing frontends (Interoperability)	DokChess can be integrated in existing graphical chess frontends with reasonable effort.
Acceptable playing strength (Attractiveness)	DokChess plays strong enough to beat weak opponents safely and at least challenges casual players.
Quick response to opponent's moves (Efficiency)	Since DokChess is used as live-demo in seminars and lectures, calculation of moves takes place quickly.

Figure 5.2: Quality goals for DokChess

The quality scenarios in section V 5.10 detail these goals and serve to evaluate their achievement.

1.3 Stakeholders

The following table illustrates the stakeholders of DokChess and their respective intentions:

Who?	Matters and concern
Software Architects	Software architects get an impression on how architecture documentation for a specific system may look like. They reproduce things (e.g. format, notation) in their daily work. They gain confidence for their own documentation tasks. Usually they have no deep knowledge about chess.
Developers	Developers accept responsibility for architectural tasks in the team. During the study of DokChess they acquire a taste for implementing a chess engine on their own. They are curious about concrete suggestions.
Stefan Zörner	Stefan needs attractive examples for his book. He uses DokChess as a case study in workshops and presentations on software design and architecture.
oose Innovative Informatik	Employers of Stefan Zörner at the time of DokChess conception. The company offers trainings, workshops and coaching on topics related to software development.

Figure 5.3: Stakeholders

V.2 Constraints

At the beginning of the project, various constraints had to be respected within the design of DokChess. They still affect the solution. This section represents these restrictions and explains – where necessary – their motivations.

2.1 Technical Constraints

The following table describes the various technical constraints encountered when using the DokChess engine:

Constraint	Background and / or motivation
Moderate hardware equipment	Operating DokChess on a standard notebook in order to show the software in the context of workshops and conferences on such a device.
Operating on Windows desktop operating systems	Standard equipment for notebooks of oose employees at the time of outlining the solution. High distribution of these operating systems at potentially interested parties (audience at conference talks, participants in trainings). Support for other operating systems (most notably Linux and Mac OS X) is desirable, but not mandatory.
Implementation in Java	Usage as an example in Java-centered trainings and Java conferences. Development with Java SE version 6 (DokChess 1.0), later Java SE 7. The engine should also run in newer Java versions, when available.
Third-party software freely available	If third-party software is involved (for example, a graphical front end), this should ideally be freely available and free of charge. The way the threshold to use it is kept low.

Figure 5.4: Technical constraints

2.2 Organizational Constraints

The following table lists the organizational constraints for building the DokChess engine:

Constraint	Background and / or motivation
Team	Stefan Zörner, supported by colleagues, friends and interested workshop or training participants
Schedule	Start of development in December 2010, first running prototype March 2011 (evening talk at oose in Hamburg), presentable version May 2011 (talk at JAX conference in Mayence, Germany). Completion of Version 1.0: February 2012 (Deadline book manuscript for 1st edition).
Process model	Risk driven development, iterative and incremental. To describe the architecture arc42 is used. An architecture documentation structured according to this template is a key project result.
Development Tools	Design with pen and paper, in addition Enterprise Architect. Work results for architecture documentation collected in Confluence Wiki. Java source code created in Eclipse or IntelliJ. However, the software can be built only with Gradle, i.e. without an IDE.
Configuration and version management	At the beginning (Version 1.0) Subversion at SourceForge, later Git at GitHub.
Test tools and test processes	JUnit 4 with annotation style both for correctness and integration testing and for compliance with efficiency targets.
Release as Open Source	The source code of the solution, or at least parts, made available as open source. License: GNU General Public License version 3.0 (GPLv3). Hosted at GitHub (https://github.com/DokChess/).

Figure 5.5: Organizational constraints

2.3 Conventions

The following are the conventions followed for building the DokChess engine:

Convention	Background and/or motivation
Architecture Documentation	Terminology and structure according to the arc42 template, version 6.0.
Coding guidelines for Java	Java coding conventions of Sun / Oracle, checked using CheckStyle
Chess-specific file formats	Use of established standards for chess-specific notations and exchange formats within the solution. Topics: moves, positions, games, openings, ... Never develop own formats here. Principle: Favour open standards over proprietary formats (which commercial programs may use).

Figure 5.6: Conventions

V.3 Context

This section describes the environment of DokChess- who are its users, and with which other systems does it interact with.

3.1 Business Context

The following figure depicts the domain perspective of DokChess:

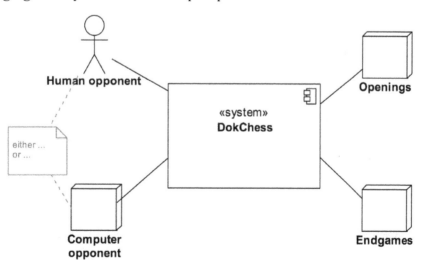

Figure 5.7: DokChess business context

The following table lists the different elements of the business context of DokChess:

Actor	Description
Human opponent (user)	Chess is played between two opponents, who move their pieces in turn. DokChess takes the role of one of the opponents, and competes against a human opponent. For this purpose, the two need to communicate, e.g. about their moves, or draw offers.
Computer opponent (external system)	As an alternative to a human opponent DokChess can also compete with a different engine. The requirements related to the exchange of information are the same.
Openings (external system)	About the opening, which is the early stage of a game, extensive knowledge exists in chess literature. This knowledge is partly free and partly also commercially available in the form of libraries and databases. Within DokChess no such library is created. Optionally an external system is connected instead in order to permit a knowledge based play in the early stages, as expected by human players.
Endgames (external system)	If just a very few pieces are left on the board (e.g. only the two kings and a queen), endgame libraries can be used analogously to opening libraries. For any position with this piece constellation these libraries include the statement whether a position is won, drawn or lost, and if possible the necessary winning move. Within DokChess no such library is created. Optionally an external system is connected instead in order to bring clearly won games home safely, or to use the knowledge from the libraries for analysis and position evaluation.

Figure 5.8: Actors of DokChess

3.2 Deployment Context

The following figure depicts the deployment perspective of DokChess:

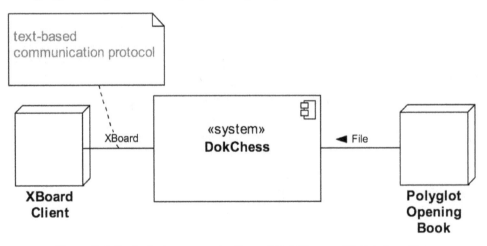

Figure 5.9: Technical communication of DokChess with third parties

The following table describes the various elements of deployment context for DokChess:

Actor	Description
XBoard client (external system)	A human player is connected to DokChess with a graphical front-end. The development of such is not part of DokChess. Each graphical frontend can be used instead, if it supports the so-called XBoard protocol. These include Xboard (or Winboard on Windows), Arena and Aquarium.
Polyglot Opening Book (external system)	Polyglot Opening Book is a binary file format for opening libraries. DokChess allows the optional connection of such books. Only read access is used.

Figure 5.10: Deployment elements for DokChess

On Endgames

The implementation of a connection to endgame databases (such as Nalimov Endgame tablebases (https://en.wikipedia.org/wiki/Endgame_tablebase)) has been dropped due to the effort of implementation (refer V 11.2 Risk: *Effort of implementation*). The design, however, is open to appropriate extensions.

V.4 Solution Strategy

The following table contrasts the quality goals of DokChess with matching architecture approaches and thus provides easy access to the solution:

Quality Goal	Matching approaches in the solution
Accessible example (Analysability)	• architectural overview structured by arc42 • explicit, object-oriented domain model • detailed documentation of public interfaces with Javadoc
Platform appealing to experiments (Changeability)	• widely spread programming language Java → (a) • Interfaces for core abstractions (for instance: position evaluation, game rules) • immutable objects (position, move, …) make implementation of many algorithms easier • "plugging" of elements with dependency injection leads to interchangeability → (b) • High test coverage as a safety net
Using existing frontends (Interoperability)	• Use of the common communication protocol XBoard, →(c) • Use of portable Java → (a)
Acceptable playing strength (Attractiveness)	• Integration of chess opening book libraries → (d) • implementation of minimax algorithm and a proper position evaluation → (e) • Integration tests with chess problems for tactics and mate positions
Quick response to opponent's moves (Efficiency)	• Reactive extensions for concurrent calculation with newly found better moves as events → (f) • Optimization of minimax by alpha-beta pruning → (e) • Efficient domain model implementation • Integration tests with time limits

Figure 5.11: Quality goals and matching approaches

> **Note**
>
> Small letters in brackets, such as (x), link individual approaches from the right-hand side of the table to the following architectural overview diagram.

The following figure presents a general overview of Dokchess architecture:

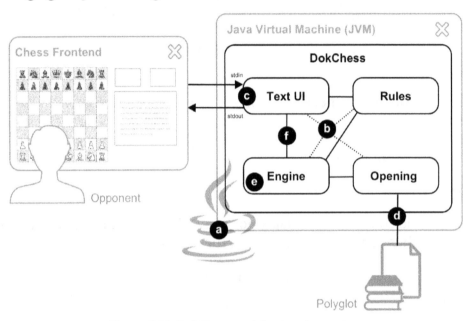

Figure 5.12: DokChess architectural overview

The remaining section V 4. introduces significant architectural aspects and refers to further information in chapter V.

4.1 Structure of DokChess

DokChess is implemented as a Java program with a main routine. It is roughly split into the following parts:

- An implementation of the rules of chess
- The engine itself, which selects the moves
- The connection to a graphical user interface via the XBoard protocol
- An adapter for a specific opening book format (Polyglot Opening Book)

This decomposition allows you to replace things such as the communication protocol or the opening book format, if necessary. All parts are abstracted through interfaces. Their implementations are assembled via dependency injection (refer V 5. Building Block View and V 8.1 Concept "Dependencies Between Modules"). The decomposition further allows the software, especially the chess algorithms, to be tested automatically (refer concept V 8.7 "Testability")..

The interaction between algorithms takes place using the exchange of data structures motivated by the domain implemented as Java classes (piece, move and so on, refer V 8.2 *Chess Domain Model*). Here, better understandability is preferred at the cost of efficiency. Nevertheless, DokChess reached an acceptable playing strength, as a run through the corresponding scenarios shows (refer V 10 Quality Scenarios).

The key element of the data structure design is the game situation. This includes the placement of the chess pieces and other aspects that belong to the position (such as which side moves next). Again, understandability is preferred to efficiency in the implementation of the class motivated by the domain. An important aspect is that, like all other domain classes, this class is immutable (refer decision V 9.2 Are position objects changeable or not?).

4.2 Game Strategy

For the integration of opening libraries, the Polyglot Opening Book file format was implemented (refer V 5 *Building Block View, Subsystem Opening (Blackbox)*). This way, DokChess responds with profound chess knowledge from the beginning.

The classic minimax algorithm (https://en.wikipedia.org/wiki/Minimax) with a fixed search depth in the game tree is responsible for the strategy as the game continues. Its basic implementation is single-threaded. The evaluation of a position at an end node in the game tree is based solely on the material mentioned in V 5.2 *Building Block View level 2, Engine (Whitebox)*. Nevertheless, these simple implementations already meet the quality scenarios under the given constraints.

Alpha-beta pruning (https://en.wikipedia.org/wiki/Alpha–beta_pruning) illustrates the simple replacement of algorithms. Playing strength and efficiency considerably improve by searching the tree more deeply within the same computation time. The immutable data structures of DokChess also facilitate implementing concurrent algorithms; a parallel minimax algorithm is included as an example.

4.3 The Connection of the Engine

DokChess has no graphical user interface. Instead, communication takes place via standard input and output. The text-based XBoard acts as a communication protocol (refer decision V 9.1 *How does the engine communicate with the outside world?*). You can use DokChess interactively with the command line if you know the XBoard commands and are able to interpret the engine responses (refer Concept V 8.3 User Interface"). See the following screenshot:

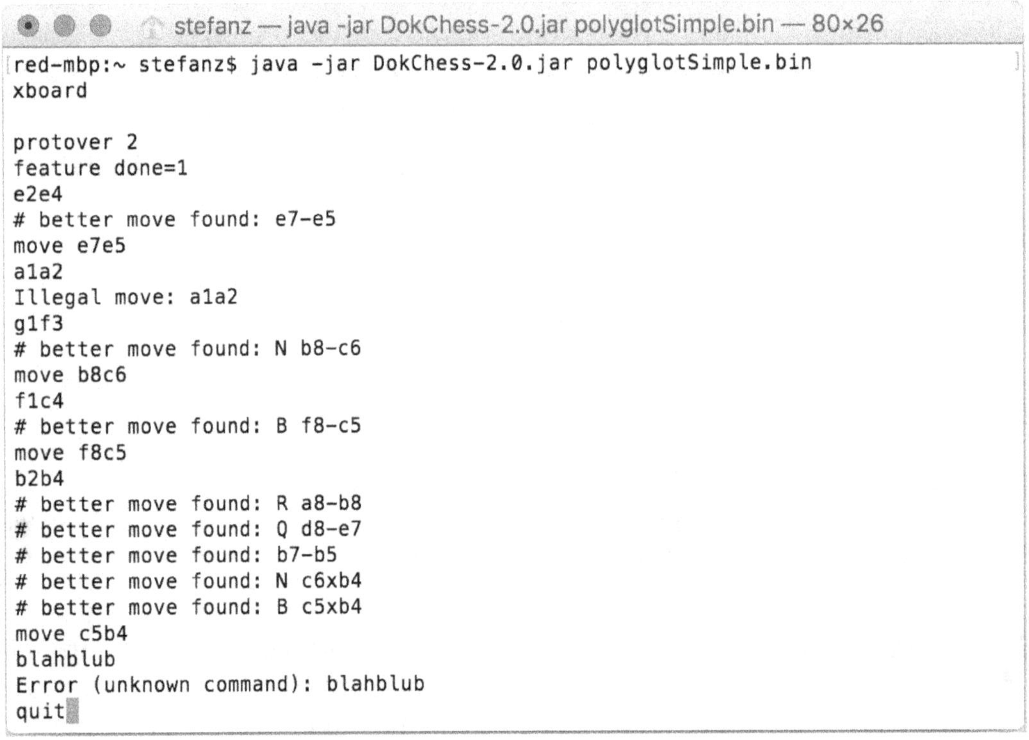

```
stefanz — java -jar DokChess-2.0.jar polyglotSimple.bin — 80×26
[red-mbp:~ stefanz$ java -jar DokChess-2.0.jar polyglotSimple.bin
xboard

protover 2
feature done=1
e2e4
# better move found: e7-e5
move e7e5
a1a2
Illegal move: a1a2
g1f3
# better move found: N b8-c6
move b8c6
f1c4
# better move found: B f8-c5
move f8c5
b2b4
# better move found: R a8-b8
# better move found: Q d8-e7
# better move found: b7-b5
# better move found: N c6xb4
# better move found: B c5xb4
move c5b4
blahblub
Error (unknown command): blahblub
quit
```

Figure 5.13: DokChess on the command line

The actual DokChess engine is attached by a reactive approach (Reactive Extensions) (refer *Runtime View*, V.6.1 Move Calculation Walkthrough). DokChess is accessible even during its analysis. This way, for instance, a user can force the engine to move immediately.

On Windows, integrating DokChess in a UI is done with a batch file (*.bat). It starts the **Java Virtual Machine** (**JVM**) with the class with the `main` method as a parameter (refer V 7. "Deployment View")..

V.5 Building Block View

This section describes the decomposition of DokChess into modules. These are also reflected in the package structure of the Java source code. In DokChess, we call modules of the first decomposition level's subsystems. The building block view level 1 presents them, including their interfaces. For the **Engine** subsystem, this overview also includes a more detailed breakdown into level 2 (refer V.6.1 *Move Determination Walkthrough* contains an example of the interaction between the subsystems at runtime).

5.1 Building Block View-Level 1

DokChess breaks down into four subsystems, as presented in the following figure.

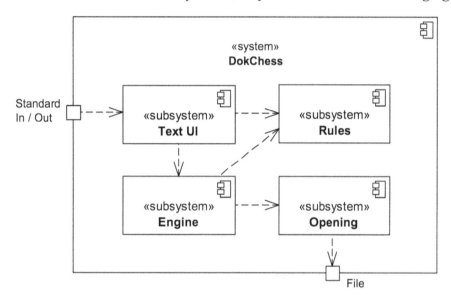

Figure 5.14: Building block view, level 1 of DokChess

The dashed arrows represent logical dependencies between the subsystems ($x \rightarrow y$ for x depends on y). The squared boxes on the membrane of the system are interaction points (ports) with the outside world (refer V.3.2 *Deployment Context*):

Subsystem	Short description
Text UI	Realizes communication with a client using the XBoard protocol.
Rules	Provides the rules of chess and for instance can determine all valid moves for a position.
Engine	Contains the determination of a next move starting from a game situation.
Opening	Provides standard moves of the chess opening literature for a game situation.

Figure 5.15: Subsystems of DokChess

5.1.1 Subsystem Text UI (Blackbox)

Intent/Responsibility

This subsystem implements the communication with a client (for example, a graphical user interface) using the text-based XBoard protocol (refer V.9.1 *Decision*). It reads commands from standard input, checks them against the rules of the game, and converts them for the **Engine**. Responses from the **Engine** (especially the moves) will be accepted by the subsystem as events, formatted according to the protocol and returned via standard output. Thus, the subsystem is driving the whole game.

Interfaces

The subsystem provides its functionality via the `org.dokchess.textui.xboard.XBoard` `Java class`:

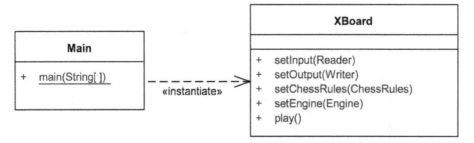

Figure 5.16: The XBoard and Main classes

The following table describes every method of the XBoard class:

Method	Short description
setInput	Set the protocol input with a dependency injection (→ Concept V.8.1). Typically, the standard input (stdin), automated tests use a different source.
setOutput	Set the protocol output. Typically, the standard output (stdout), automated tests may use a different target.
setChessRules	Sets an implementation of the game rules, → V.5.1.2 "Subsystem Rules (Black Box)"
setEngine	Sets an implementation of the engine, → V.5.1.3 "Subsystem Engine (Black Box)"
play	Starts the actual communication (input / processing / output) in a infinite loop until the quit command.

Figure 5.17: XBoard methods

Files

The implementation is located below the packages

org.dokchess.textui...

Open Issues

The implementation of the XBoard protocol is incomplete. Nevertheless, it is sufficient for the requirements of DokChess. But, in particular, the following features are not supported:

- Time control

- Permanent brain (thinking while the opponent thinks)

- Draw offers and the opponent giving up

- Chess variants (alternative rules, such as Chess960)

5.1.2 Subsystem Rules (Blackbox)

Intent/Responsibility

This subsystem accounts for the rules of chess according to the *International Chess Federation (FIDE)*. It determines all valid moves for a position and decides whether it is a check, a checkmate, or a stalemate.

Interfaces

The subsystem provides its functionality via the **org.dokchess.rules.ChessRules** Java interface.

The default implementation of the interface is the **org.dokchess.rules. DefaultChessRules** class:

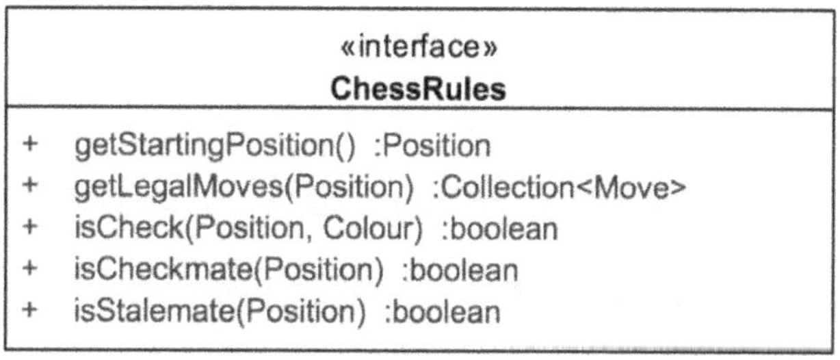

```
              «interface»
              ChessRules
  +  getStartingPosition() :Position
  +  getLegalMoves(Position) :Collection<Move>
  +  isCheck(Position, Colour) :boolean
  +  isCheckmate(Position) :boolean
  +  isStalemate(Position) :boolean
```

Figure 5.18: The ChessRules interface

The following table describes every method used in the interface:

Method	Short description
getStartingPosition	Returns the starting position of the game. White begins.
getLegalMoves	Returns the set of all legal moves for a given position. The current player is determined from the position parameter. In case of a mate or stalemate an empty collection is the result. Thus the method never returns null.
isCheck	Checks whether the king of the given colour is attacked by the opponent.
isCheckmate	Checks whether the given position is a mate. I.e. the king of the current player is under attack, and no legal move changes this. The player to move has lost the game.
isStalemate	Checks whether the given position is a stalemate. I.e. the current player has no valid move, but the king is not under attack. The game is considered a draw.

Figure 5.19: ChessRules methods with short descriptions

Concept V 8.2 Chess domain model describes the types used in the interface as call and return parameters (**Move**, **Position**, **Colour**). Refer to the source code documentation (javadoc) for more details.

Files

The implementation is located below the packages

org.dokchess.rules...

Open Issues

Apart from the stalemate, the subsystem cannot recognize any draw. In particular, the following rules are not implemented (refer, V.11.2 *Risk: Effort of implementation*):

- 50 moves rule
- Threefold repetition

5.1.3 Subsystem Engine (Blackbox)

Intent/Responsibility

This subsystem contains the determination of the next move in a particular game position. The position is given from an external entity. The engine itself is stateful and always plays one game at a time. The default implementation needs an implementation of the game rules to work. An opening library, however, is optional.

Interfaces

The **Engine** subsystem provides its functionality via the org.dokchess.engine.Engine Java interface.

The default implementation is the **org.dokchess.engine.DefaultEngine** class:

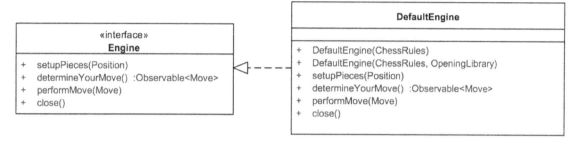

Figure 5.20: The Engine interface and the DefaultEngine class

The methods of the **Engine** interface are described as follows:

Method	Short description
setupPieces	Sets the state of the engine to the specified position. If currently a move calculation is running, this will be cancelled.
determineYourMove	Starts the determination of a move for the current game situation. Returns move candidates asynchronously via an Observable (→ Runtime View V.6.1 "Move Determination Walkthrough"). The engine does not perform the moves.
performMove	Performs the move given, which changes the state of the engine. If currently a movecalculation is running, this will be canceled.
close	Closes the engine. The method makes it possible to free resources. No move calculations are allowed afterwards.

Figure 5.21: Methods of Engine interface

Methods of the **DefaultEngine** class (in addition to the **Engine** interface) are listed as follows:

Method	Short description
DefaultEngine	Constructors set an implementation of the chess rules, → V.5.1.2 Subsystem Rules (Black Box) and an (optional) opening book, whose moves will be preferred to own considerations → V.5.1.4 Subsystem Opening (Black Box).

Figure 5.22: DefaultEngine method

Concept V 8.2 Chess Domain Model describes the types used in the interface as call and return parameters (**Move** and **Position**). Refer to the source code documentation (*Javadoc*) for more information.

Files

The implementation of the **Engine** subsystem and corresponding unit tests are located below the following packages:

org.dokchess.engine...

5.1.4 Subsystem Opening (Blackbox)

Intent/Responsibility

This subsystem provides opening libraries and implements the **PolyglotOpeningBook** format. This format is currently the only one available, which is not proprietary. Corresponding book files and associated tools are freely available on the internet.

Interfaces

The Opening subsystem provides its functionality via the **org.dokchess.opening. OpeningLibrary** Java interface.

The **org.dokchess.opening.polyglot.PolyglotOpeningBook** class provides one possible implementation:

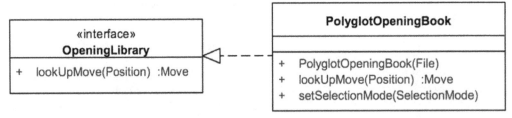

Figure 5.23: Interface OpeningLibrary and PolyglotOpeningBook class

Here is the method of the `OpeningLibrary` interface:

`lookUpMove`: Returns a standard move for the specified position from the library, or null.

The **PolyglotOpeningBook** class is an adapter for the **PolyglotOpeningBook** file format. Implementation of `OpeningLibrary` reads a binary file in the appropriate format and returns a move to the specified position, if the library contains any.

Here are the methods of the **PolyglotOpeningBook** class (in addition to the OpeningLibrary interface):

Method	Short description
PolyglotOpeningBook	Constructor, expects the input file.
setSelectionMode	Sets the mode to select a move, if there is more than one candidate in the library for the given position.

Figure 5.24: Method of the PolyglotOpeningBook class

Concept V 8.2 Chess domain model describes the types used in the interface as `call` and `return` parameters (`Move` and `Position`). Refer to the source code documentation (**Javadoc**) for more information.

Files

The implementation, unit tests, and test data for the Polyglot file format are located below the following packages:

org.dokchess.opening...

Open Issues

Following are the open issues encountered:

- The implemented options for move selection from the **PolyglotOpeningBook** in the case of several candidates are limited (the first, the most often played, by chance).

- The implementation cannot handle multiple library files at the same time. It cannot, therefore, mix them to combine the knowledge.

5.2 Level 2: Engine (Whitebox)

The **Engine** breaks down into the **Search** and (position) **Evaluation** modules, as shown in the following diagram. If available, the determination of the move is initially delegated to an opening book. **Search** is only used if the book does not provide a standard move:

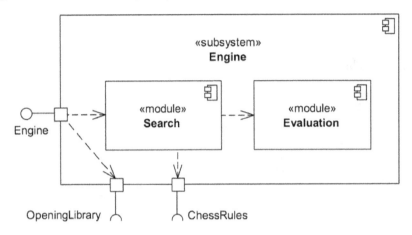

Figure 5.25: Engine, building block view, level 2

The following list describes the modules in level 2 engine:

- **Search**: Determines the optimal move for a position under certain conditions

- **Evaluation**: Evaluates a position from an opponent's perspective.

5.2.1 Search (Blackbox)

Intent/Responsibility

The module determines the optimal move for a position under certain conditions. In the game of chess, an optimal move always exists, theoretically. The high number of possible moves and the resultingly incredible number of game situations to consider makes it impossible to determine the optimal move in practice. Common algorithms such as Minimax explore the game tree only up to a certain depth.

Interfaces

The module provides its functionality via the **org.dokchess.engine.search.Search** Java interface.

The **org.dokchess.engine.search.MinimaxAlgorithm** class implements the interface with the Minimax algorithm. The **MinimaxParallelSearch** class uses the algorithm and implements the same **Search** interface. It examines several subtrees concurrently; if it finds a better move, the caller receives an **onNext** message via the observer pattern. The **Search** indicates the completion of its work with an **onComplete** message:

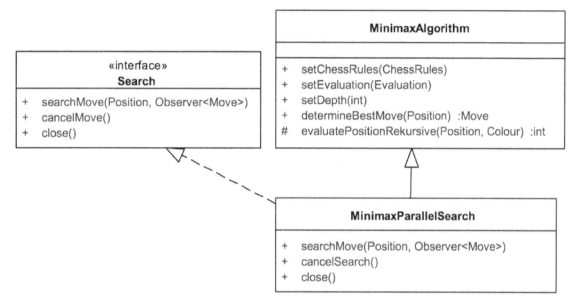

Figure 5.26: The Search interface and the MinimaxAlgorithm and MinimaxParallelSearch classes

Here are the methods of the **Search** interface:

Method	Short description
searchMove	Starts a search for a move on the specified position. Returns gradually better moves as events on the passed observer. The end of the search (no better move found) is also signaled to the observer.
cancelSearch	Cancels the current search.
close	Closes the search completely. No moves may be determined after calling this method.

Figure 5.27: Methods of Search interface

Here are the methods of the **MinimaxAlgorithm** class:

Method	Short description
setEvaluation	Set the evaluation function on which the positions are rated when the maximum search depth is reached.→ V.5.2.2 "Module Evaluation (Black Box)"
setChessRules	setChessRules Sets an implementation of the chess rules via dependency injection, → V.5.1.2 "Subsystem Rules (Black Box)"
setDepth	Set the maximum search depth in half moves. That means at 4 each player moves twice.
determineBestMove	Determines the optimal move according to minimax for the position passed and given evaluation at fixed search depth. The method blocks and is deterministic.

Figure 5.28: Methods of the **MinimaxAlgorithm** class

Files

The implementation is located below the packages **org.dokchess.engine.search**.

5.2.2 Evaluation (Blackbox)

Intent/Responsibility

The module evaluates a position from the opponent's perspective. The result is a number, and 0 is a balanced situation. A positive number describes an advantage for the player and a negative number is a disadvantage. The higher the number, the greater the advantage or disadvantage. The module makes it therefore possible to compare positions with each other.

Interfaces

The Evaluation module provides its functionality via the **org.dokchess.engine.eval. Evaluation** Java interface.

The **org.dokchess.engine.eval.StandardMaterialEvaluation** class is a very simple implementation. The interface contains constants for typical ratings:

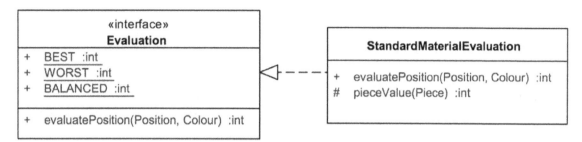

Figure 5.29: The Evaluation interface and StandardMaterialEvaluation class

Here is a method of the Evaluation interface:

evaluatePosition: Returns an evaluation value for the given position from the view of the specified player's color. The higher the better.

The **StandardMaterialEvaluation** implementation class takes only the present pieces (material) into account. Each piece type has a value (pawn 1, knight 3, ..., queen 9). The pieces on the board are added accordingly. The player's figures are positive, and the opponent's pieces are negative. Accordingly, with balanced material, the result is 0. If you lose a queen, the value drops by 9.

Files

The implementation is located below the packages *org.dokchess.engine.eval*.

Open Issues

In the pure material evaluation, it does not matter where the pieces stand. A pawn in its starting position is worth as much as a pawn that's just short of promotion. And a knight on the edge corresponds to a knight in the center. There is plenty of room for improvement, which has not been exploited because DokChess should have invited others to experiment.

V.6 Runtime View

In contrast to the static building block view, this section visualizes dynamic aspects. How do the pieces work together?

6.1 Move Determination Walkthrough

After establishing the XBoard protocol, the client (white) starts a game by indicating a move. The following sequence diagram shows an example interaction at the subsystem level from the input, "**e2e4**" (white pawn e2-e4), to DokChess' response, which is the output "move **b8c6**" (*black knight b8-c6, the "Nimzowitsch defense"* (https://en.wikipedia. org/wiki/Nimzowitsch_Defence)):

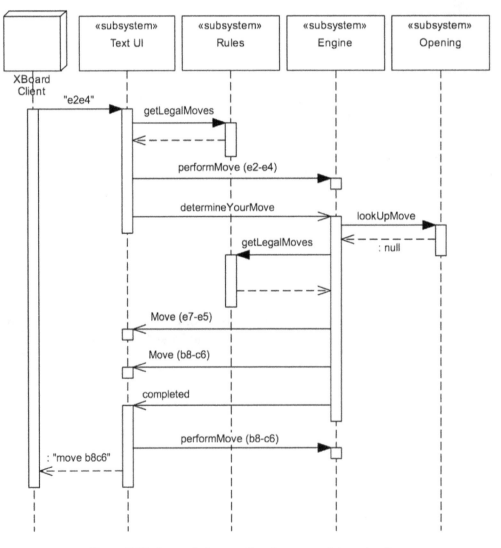

Figure 5.30: Example interaction for move determination

First, the Text UI subsystem validates the input with the aid of the **Rules** subsystem (refer V 8.4, *Plausibility Checks and Validation*). The move in the example is recognized as legal and performed on the (stateful) **Engine** (the `performMove` message) afterward. Then, the Text UI subsystem asks the **Engine** to determine its move. Since move computation can take a long time, but DokChess should still continue to react to inputs, this call is asynchronous. The engine comes back with possible moves.

The **Engine** examines at first whether the opening book has something to offer. In the example, this is not the case. The **Engine** has to calculate the move on its own. It then accesses the **Rules** and determines all valid moves as candidates. Afterward, it investigates and rates them and gradually reports better moves (better from the perspective of the **Engine**) back to the caller (the Text UI subsystem). Here, the observer pattern is used (implementation with reactive extensions (http://reactivex.io/intro.html)).

The example diagram shows that two moves have been found (pawn **e7-e5** and knight **b8-c6**) and finally the message that the search is complete, so the engine does not provide better moves. The Text UI subsystem takes the last move of the **Engine** and prints it as a string to standard output according to the XBoard protocol: "move **b8c6**".

V.7 Deployment View

This view describes the operation of DokChess. As a Java program, it is relatively undemanding if you want to use it only on the command line. However, this is inconvenient and requires a physical chessboard with coordinates if the user cannot play blindfolded. Therefore, here is an explanation of how to configure DokChess in conjunction with a graphical frontend.

7.1 Windows Infrastructure

The following deployment diagram shows the use of DokChess on Windows without an opening book. Arena is used as an example frontend (refer V 9.1, *decision How does the engine communicate with the outside world?*):

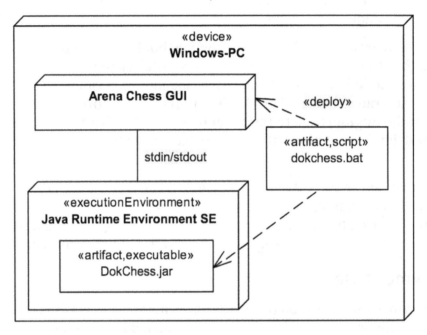

Figure 5.31: Deploying DokChess on a Windows PC

Software requirements on a PC are as folllows:

- Java Runtime Environment SE 7 (or higher).

- The JVM (*javaw.exe*) is in the path otherwise adapt **dokchess.bat**.

- Arena (http://www.playwitharena.de).

DokChess.jar contains the compiled Java source code of all the modules and all the necessary dependencies (Uber-jar). The **dokchess.bat** script file starts the JVM with DokChess. Both are available on the computer in a common directory because **dokchess.bat** addresses the JAR file.

Within Arena, the script file is declared in the following menu: **Engine | Install a new Engine**. You will see a file selection. The file type can be limited to *** .bat** files. Then, set the engine type to WinBoard. In other chess frontends, declaring an engine is very similar. See the corresponding documentation for details.

V.8 Technical and Cross cutting Concepts

This section describes general structures and system-wide aspects. It also presents various technical solutions.

8.1 Dependencies between Modules

DokChess invites developers to experiment and to extend the engine (V 1.2 *Quality Goals*). In order to do so, the modules are loosely coupled. DokChess modules are implementations of Java interfaces. Java classes that require parts signal this with appropriate methods `set"Module"("Interface" …)`. They don't take care of resolving a dependency, for instance, by using a factory. Instead, the client resolves the dependencies by creating suitable implementations with `new` and putting them together with setter methods, also known as **Dependency Injection** (**DI**).

Interfaces and DI enable alternative implementations within DokChess. Adding functionality with the help of the decorator pattern (**Gamma+94**) is possible as well. Furthermore, **aspect-oriented programming** (**AOP**) solutions, which rely on Java dynamic proxies, are applicable interfaces. Plus, this handling of dependencies positively affects testability (refer V 8.7, *Concept Testability*).

DokChess abstains from the use of a concrete DI framework. The modules are hard-wired in the code, however, only in unit tests and glue code (for example, the `main` class). No annotation-driven configuration is present in the code.

This gives adventurous developers free choice regarding a specific DI implementation. Since the Java modules are pure **Plain Old Java Objects** (**POJOs**), nothing prevents configuration with the Spring Framework, for example, or **Contexts and Dependency Injection** (**CDI**) for the Java EE Platform.

8.2 Chess Domain Model

"The game of chess is played between two opponents who move their pieces on a square board called a 'chessboard." - FIDE Laws of Chess

The different modules of DokChess exchange chess-specific data. This includes the game situation on the chessboard (position), for instance, as well as opponents' and engines' moves. All interfaces use the same domain objects as `call` and `return` parameters.

This section contains a brief overview of these data structures and their relationships. All the classes and enumeration types (enums) are located in the `org.dokchess.domain` package. See the source documentation (Javadoc) for details.

A chess piece is characterized by color (black or white) and type (king, queen, and so on). In the DokChess domain model, a piece does not know its location on the board. The `Piece` class is immutable, and so are all other domain classes:

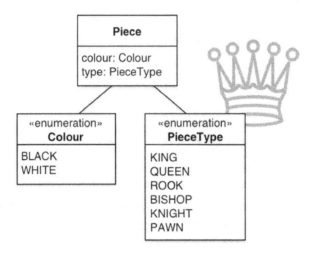

Figure 5.32: Chess pieces attributes

A chessboard consists of 8 x 8 squares, which are arranged in 8 rows called ranks (1-8) and 8 columns called files (a-h). The `Square` class describes one of these. Since a square can be occupied by only one piece, source and target squares are sufficient to specify a move (the `Move` class). The only exception is the promotion of a pawn on the opponent's baseline. Here, the player decides which piece type they want to convert the pawn to (typically, but not necessarily, a queen). Castling moves are represented as king moves over two squares in the corresponding direction. The additional attributes for the moving piece and whether the move is a capture are useful for the analysis tasks of the engine:

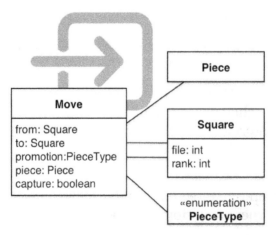

Figure 5.33: A move from square to square

The **Position** class describes the current situation on the board. In particular, these are the piece locations on the board, which are internally represented as a two-dimensional array (**8 x 8**). If a square is not occupied, **null** is stored in the array. To complete the game situation, the **Position** class includes information about which side moves next, which castlings are still possible (if any), and whether capturing en passant is allowed:

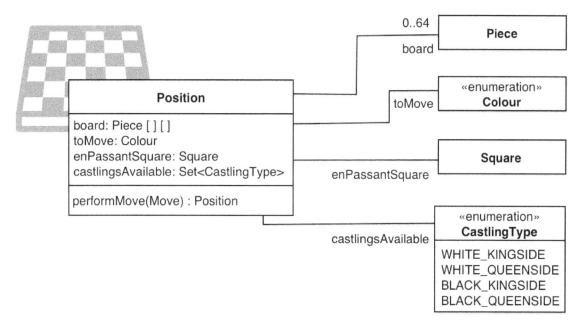

Figure 5.34: A position describes a game state

The **Position** class is immutable as well. Therefore, the **performMove()** method returns a new position with the modified game situation (refer V 9.2 *decision, Are position objects changeable or not?*).

8.3 User Interface

DokChess has no graphical user interface. It interacts via the XBoard protocol with the outside world (refer V 9.1, *decision How does the engine communicate with the outside world?*).

The XBoard protocol is text-based. If you have mastered the main DokChess commands in a command line (Unix shell, or the Windows Command Prompt), you can interact with the engine. The following table shows a sample dialog. All commands are terminated with a new line. By default, the engine plays black pieces. You can change this with the `white` command of XBoard:

Client → DokChess	DokChess → Client	Comments
xboard		client wants to use the XBoard-Protocol (required since engines party understand other, sometimes even multiple protocols)
protover 2	feature done=1	protocol version 2 line by line notification of additional features of the engine (here: none)
e2e4	move b8c6	white plays pawn e2-e42 black (DokChess) plays knight b8-c6 client ends the game (DokChess terminates)
quit		

Figure 5.35: DokChess sample dialog

Mann+2009 (https://www.gnu.org/software/xboard/engine-intf.html) describes the protocol in detail. In DokChess, the Text UI subsystem is responsible for the protocol implementation (*refer Building Block View, V 5.1.2, Subsystem Text UI (Blackbox)*).

A more typical use of DokChess is a graphical chess frontend such as Arena (as shown in the following screenshot). It accepts the moves of the opponent in a comfortable interface, passes them to DokChess in the form of XBoard commands (as shown in the preceding table (the **Client | DokChess** column), and translates the answers (the **DokChess | Client** column) graphically:

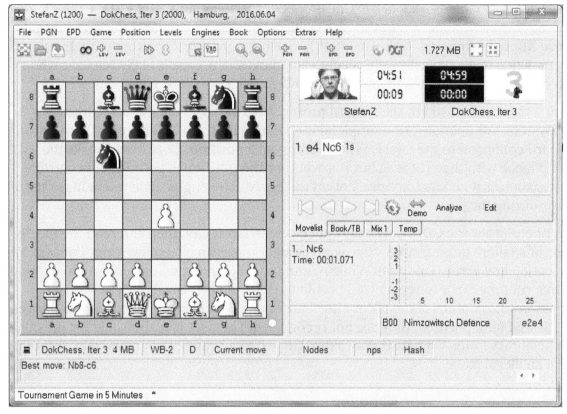

Figure 5.36: DokChess combined with the Arena chess frontend on Windows

8.4 Plausibility Checks and Validation

In simple terms, DokChess is an algorithm. It responds to the moves of the opponent with its own moves. Two channels are relevant to input validation:

- The XBoard protocol for interactive user input from the opponent

- Opening libraries in the form of files

Input that comes through the Xboard protocol is parsed from the corresponding subsystem. In the case of unknown or unimplemented commands, DokChess reports the Xboard **Error** command to the client.

If a move command is issued, DokChess checks the rules subsystem to see whether the move is allowed or not. In the case of illegal moves, DokChess reports the Illegal move XBoard command to the client. When using a graphical frontend, this should not occur, since these typically only accept valid moves. The case is likely relevant when interacting via the command line (*refer Concept V 8.3 User Interface*).

Inputs that come through the XBoard protocol are parsed from the corresponding subsystem. For unknown or unimplemented commands, DokChess reports the Error XBoard command to the client. When setting up a position, DokChess checks the compliance with the protocol, but not whether the position is permitted. In extreme cases (such as if no kings are present on the board), the engine subsystem may raise an error during the game.

For opening libraries, DokChess only checks whether it can open and read the file. In case of a failure (for example, `file not found`), it raises an exception (refer concept V.8.5 *Exception and Error Handling*). While reading the file, the opening subsystem responds with a runtime error to recognized problems (for example, `invalid file format`). However, the content of the library itself is not checked. For example, if invalid moves are stored for a position, they are not recognized. The user is responsible for the quality of the library (refer V 3.1 *Business Context*). In extreme cases, the engine may respond with an illegal move.

8.5 Exception and Error Handling

DokChess has no user interface of its own. Therefore, it must indicate problems to the outside world.

All DokChess subsystem methods throw runtime exceptions. In addition, *Engine subsystem error messages (onError)* may occur during an asynchronous search. Your own extensions (for example, a custom search) must be implemented accordingly. Checked exceptions (for example, `java.io.IOException`) need to be wrapped in runtime exceptions.

The Javadoc of methods and constructors in question shows the rare cases where exceptions are expected in DokChess, such as difficulty with reading or opening a book file, or when trying move calculations within the engine at an invalid position (if identified). All other exceptions would be programming errors (please report them at https://github.com/DokChess/).

The XBoard subsystem catches all exceptions and communicates them via the XBoard protocol outwards (using the **tellusererror** command). A graphical frontend usually visualizes them in an error dialog or alert box. The following screenshot depicts that for the Arena chess frontend:

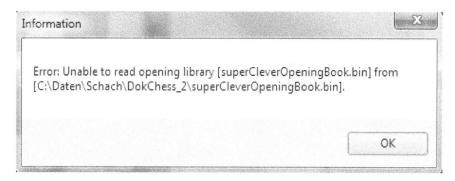

Figure 5.37: An error dialog in Arena

DokChess continues to work normally. The client decides whether proceeding in this specific situation makes sense. For example, it could continue to play without an opening book.

8.6 Logging and Tracing

For improvements and extensions, the analysis capabilities provided by DokChess are of note, particularly in case of an error.

The DokChess functionality can be checked easily with unit tests. This is particularly true for the correct implementation of the game rules and for the gameplay of the engine (refer V 8.7, *Testability*). It holds true for your own extensions in this area as well.

Therefore, there is no fine-grained logging output within DokChess. Solutions such as SLF4J (https://www.slf4j.org) are not present. In this way, we avoid dependency on an external library, and the source code is not polluted by this aspect at all.

For communication between the client and DokChess via the XBoard protocol, in addition to interactive operations via a shell (refer, Concept V 8.3 *User Interface*), the client may monitor the conversation. Common chess frontends permit this by writing log files and/or a simultaneous display of a log window during the game. The following screenshot shows this functionality within Arena:

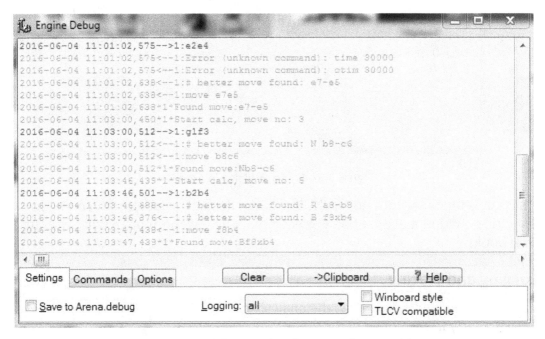

Figure 5.38: Log and debug window for XBoard protocol in Arena

If the engine blocks and it is unclear what went on the XBoard protocol, such tools are simply invaluable. Due to the availability of this feature, communication protocol tracing was not implemented within DokChess at all.

8.7 Testability

Nothing is more embarrassing for an engine than an illegal move.

The functionality of the individual modules of DokChess is ensured by extensive unit tests. You find a **src/test** folder next to **src/main**, where the Java source code of the modules is stored. It mirrors the package structure, and in the corresponding packages, unit tests for the classes are implemented with JUnit 4 (https://junit.org/junit4/).

Standard unit testing, which examines individual classes, is named after the class itself with the suffix **Test**. In addition, there are tests that examine the interaction of modules, and in extreme cases, the whole system. With the help of such tests, the correct playing of DokChess is ensured. More complex, long-running integration tests are in **src/integTest**. This includes playing entire games.

In many tests, positions must be provided as call parameters. Here, the **Forsyth-Edwards Notation** (**FEN**) is used. This notation allows the specification of a complete game scenario as a compact string without a line break and is therefore perfect for use in automated tests.

The starting position in FEN is as follows:

```
"rnbqkbnr/pppppppp/8/8/8/8/PPPPPPPP/RNBQKBNR w KQkq - 0 1"
```

Lowercase letters stand for black pieces, and uppercase letters stand for white pieces. For the piece types, the initials of the English names (r for rook, p for pawn, and so on) are used:

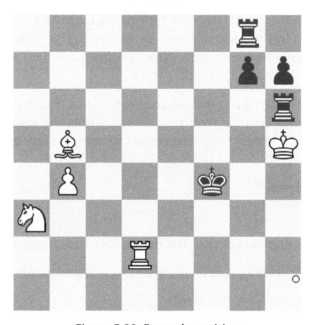

Figure 5.39: Example position

The game situation in the preceding diagram, with white before its 79th move, with 30 half-moves long no piece was captured and no pawn was moved, looks like this in FEN:

```
"6r1/6pp/7r/1B5K/1P3k2/N7/3R4/8 w - - 30 79"
```

And it reads 6 squares free, black rook, square free, new rank ....

Details about the notation can be found on Wikipedia at https://en.wikipedia.org/wiki/Forsyth–Edwards_Notation. The **Position** class has a constructor that accepts a string in FEN. The **toString** method of this class also provides FEN.

V.9 Design Decisions

This section enables you to understand two fundamental design decisions of DokChess in detail.

9.1 How Does the Engine Communicate with the Outside World?

Problem Background

As a central requirement, DokChess must work together with existing chess frontends. How do we connect them?

A whole series of graphical user interfaces are available for playing against chess programs. Moreover, there are software solutions with a larger scope for chess enthusiasts. In addition to the game *Human vs. Machine*, they offer more functionality, such as analyzing games. Over time, new chess programs will be released – and others will possibly disappear from the market.

Depending on how the connection with such programs is realized, DokChess can or cannot communicate with specific frontend clients. Thus, the issue affects DokChess' interoperability with existing chess software and its adaptability to future chess software.

Influences on the Decision

Constraints

The following are the constraints that influence the decisions for designing:

- Operation of the frontend at least on Windows desktop operating systems
- Support for freely available frontends
- Favoring established (chess) standards (see V 2.3 *Conventions*)

Significantly Affected Quality Attributes

- Using existing frontends (see V 1.2 *Interoperability, Quality Goals*)
- Platform appealing to experiments (see V 1.2 *Changeability, Quality goals*)
- Adaptability to future chess software

Affected Risks

Connecting to a frontend is a considerable risk (see V 11.1 *Risks*).

Assumptions

The investigation of just a few available frontends leads to all interesting integration options.

Considered Alternatives

In early 2011, the following chess frontends were investigated:

- Arena Chess GUI (available for free, runs on Windows)
- Fritz for Fun (commercially provided by ChessBase GmbH, runs on Windows)
- WinBoard/XBoard (Open source, runs on Windows, Mac OS X, *nix)

As a result, two communication protocols have been identified as options:

- **Option 1**: UCI Protocol (**universal chess interface**), see *MeyerKahlen2004*
- **Option 2**: XBoard protocol (also known as Winboard and as Chess Engine Communication Protocol), see *Mann+2009*

Neither of the two protocols are formally specified, but both are publicly documented. Both protocols are text-based, and communication between the frontend and the engine is via stdin/stdout. In both cases, the frontend starts the engine in a separate process.

The following table compares the three investigated frontends to their implemented protocols:

.	Arena 2	Fritz for fun	Winboard/ XBoard
UCI	Yes	Yes	-
XBoard-Protocol	Yes	-	Yes

Figure 5.40: Frontend comparison

Decision

Under the given constraints, the quality goals can generally be achieved with both options. Depending on which protocol is implemented, different frontends are supported.

The decision in favor of the XBoard protocol was made in early 2011. The structure of DokChess allows us to add alternative communication protocols (UCI or other) without having to change the engine itself. See dependencies in the building block view (refer V 5.1, *Building Block View, Level 1*).

The preferred frontend for Windows is Arena. It is freely available and excels the functionality of WinBoard. It has good debugging facilities. For example, it can present the communication between the frontend and the engine live in a window. Arena supports both protocols.

By opting for the XBoard protocol, other operating systems (in addition to Windows, especially Mac OS X and Linux) are also supported with freely available frontends (see the preceding table). As such, a larger circle of interested developers may use the engine, which was finally essential.

9.2 Are Position Objects Changeable or Not?

Problem Background

For various DokChess modules, game situations on the chessboard (so-called positions) must be provided and exchanged between them. Do we make the associated data structure changeable or unchangeable (immutable)?

During a game, the position changes when the opposing players move their pieces. In addition, the engine performs possible moves in its analysis, tries to counter the moves of the opponent, evaluates the outcoming positions, and then discards moves. The result is a tree that contains many thousands of different positions, depending on the search depth.

Depending on whether the position is immutable as a data structure or not, algorithms are easier or more difficult to implement, and its execution is efficient in a different way.

All modules depend on the position interface. A subsequent change would affect all of DokChess.

Influences on the Decision

Constraints

- Implementation in Java (refer V 2.1 *Technical Constraints*)
- Moderate hardware equipment (refer V 2.1 *Technical Constraints*)

Significantly Affected Quality Attributes

- Platform appealing to experiments (changeability, refer to V 1.2 *Quality Goals*)
- Acceptable playing strength (attractiveness, refer to V 1.2 *Quality Goals*)
- Quick response to opponent's moves (efficiency, refer to V 1.2 *Quality Goals*)

Affected Risks

- Effort of implementation (see V 11.2 *Risks*)

- Reaching the playing strength (see V 11.3 *Risks*)

Assumptions

- It is possible to implement a data structure with a fine-grained object model (that is, classes such as **Piece** and **Move**) that is efficient enough to provide the required playing strength within an adequate response time.

- In the future, concurrent algorithms should be implemented with the data structure as well.

Considered Alternatives

The starting point is domain-driven classes for **square**, **piece**, and **move** (refer V 8.2, *Chess Domain Model*). These classes are realized immutable as value objects (the e4 field always remains e4 after its construction).

For the position, two alternatives are considered:

- **Option (1): The position is changeable**: Individual methods of the interface, for example, performing moves or taking them back, change the object state.

  The Pseudocode for option 1 is as follows:

  ```
  Position p = new Position(); // starting position, white side to move
  p.performMove(e2e4);      // king's pawn advances two squares, black\
  to move
  p.takeBackLastMove()      // starting position again
  ```

- **Option (2): The position is unchangeable (immutable)**: That means a method for performing a move provides the new position (it copies the old one, then the move happens) as another immutable object as the result.

  The Pseudocode for option 2 is as follows:

  ```
  Position p = new Position();
  newPosition = p.performMove(e2e4); // p keeps unchanged
  ```

The following table summarizes the strengths and weaknesses of the two options:

.	(1) changeable	(2) unchangeable
Implementation effort	(-) higher	(+) lower
Efficiency (memory consumption)	(+) more economical	(-) higher demand
Efficiency (time behaviour)	(o) neutral	(-) worse
Suitability for concurrent algorithms	(-) bad	(+) good

Figure 5.41: Strengths and weaknesses

Option (1): The Position is Changeable

(+) Positive Arguments

The position with its extensive state is not copied in each move. This saves memory and CPU time, and it treats the garbage collector with care. For analysis algorithms, however, it is necessary to implement functionality that takes back the effect of moves (undo). This **Undo** also takes time, hence the neutral rating for the time behavior.

(-) Negative Arguments

The implementation of an **Undo** functionality is complex. Not only does it have to set up captured pieces back on the board, the castling rule and en passant require special treatment as well. The **Gamma+94** command pattern suggests itself as an option. The use of that pattern within algorithms is also more complex because the latter must explicitly call methods to take back the moves.

Finally, changeable state has drawbacks related to concurrency.

Option (2): The Position is Unchangeable

(+) Positive Arguments

When you perform a move, the position is copied. It does not change the original position. This eliminates the implementation of move reversal (**Undo**). Clients can simply store the old position as a value. This saves effort in the implementation compared to **option (1)**.

Immutable objects offer significant advantages in concurrent algorithms.

(-) *Negative Arguments*

Copying the state for each new position takes time. When analyzing situations, it covers many positions, which can take a lot of time.

Beyond that, copying the state for each new position costs memory. The implementation of search algorithms with backtracking at least prevents complete game trees from ending up on the heap. Nevertheless, more memory is required, and the garbage collector has more work to do.

Both points have a negative effect on efficiency.

Decision

The decision for the unchangeable position (**option 2**) was made in early 2011 due to the advantages in terms of ease of implementation and the prospect of exploiting concurrency. All the disadvantages of **option 2** are related to efficiency.

Due to the risk of failing to achieve the objectives with respect to the playing strength in an acceptable computing time (attractiveness, efficiency), prototypes of both versions have been implemented and compared in a mate search (checkmate in three moves) with the minimax algorithm. With **option 2**, the search took 30% longer, assuming you implement copying efficiently. But this option met the constraints as well.

Further optimization options could reduce the efficiency disadvantage compared with **option 1**, if necessary. But they have not been implemented in the first run in order to keep the implementation simple.

These options included the use of multiple processors/cores with concurrent algorithms. In the meantime (with DokChess 2.0), this was illustrated with a parallel minimax example.

V.10 Quality Scenarios

The quality scenarios in this section depict the fundamental quality goals of DokChess as well as other required quality properties. They allow the evaluation of decision alternatives.

10.1 Utility Tree

The following diagram gives an overview of the relevant quality attributes and their associated scenarios:

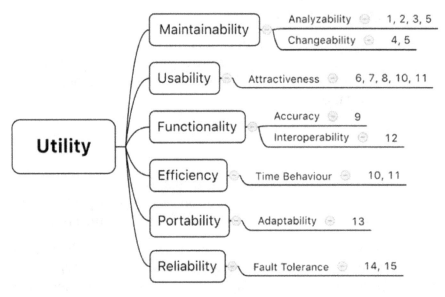

Figure 5.42: Utility Tree

10.2 Evaluation Scenarios

The evaluation scenarios can be listed as follows:

1. A person with basic knowledge of UML and chess looks for an introduction to the DokChess architecture. They get the idea of the solution strategy and the essential design within 15 minutes.

2. An architect wishes to apply arc42 searches to a concrete example for an arbitrary section of the template. They find the relevant content immediately in the documentation.

3. An experienced Java developer searches for the implementation of a module described in the design. They find it in the source code without detours or help from others.

4. A developer implements a new position evaluation. They integrate it into the existing strategies without modification and without compilation of existing source code.

5. A developer implements a piece-centric bitboard representation of the game situation. The effort (which includes replacing the existing, square-centric representation) is lower than one person week.

6. A weak player is in a game against the engine. The player moves a piece to an unguarded position, which is being attacked by the engine. The engine consequently takes the dropped piece.

7. Within a chess match, a mate in two unfolds to the engine. The engine moves safely to win the game.

8. Within a chess match, a knight fork to gain the queen or a rook arises for the engine. The engine gains the queen (or the rook) in exchange for the knight.

9. In a game situation, the engine has one or more rule-compliant moves to choose from. It plays one of them.

10. During the game, the engine responds to the move of the opponent with its own move within 5 seconds.

11. An engine integrated in a graphical frontend plays as black, and the human player begins. The engine responds within 10 seconds with its first move, and the user gets a message that the engine "thinks" within 5 seconds.

12. A user plans to use DokChess with a frontend that supports a communication protocol that's already implemented by the solution. The integration does not require any programming effort. The configuration with the frontend is carried out and tested within 10 minutes.

13. A Java programmer plans to use a chess frontend that allows the integration of engines, but does not support any of the protocols implemented by DokChess. The new protocol can be implemented without changing the existing code, and the engine can then be integrated as usual.

14. During the game, the engine receives an invalid move. The engine rejects this move and allows the input of another move thereafter and plays on in an error-free way.

15. The engine receives an illegal position to start the game. The behavior of the engine is undefined, canceling of the game is allowed, as well as invalid moves.

V.11 Risks

The following risks have been identified at the beginning of the project (December 2010). They influenced the planning of the first three iterations significantly. Since the completion of the third iteration, the risks are mastered. This architectural overview shows the risks, including the former eventuality planning, because of their large impact on the solution.

11.1 Risk: Connecting to a Frontend

There is no knowledge about connecting an engine to an existing chess frontend. Available open source engines are programmed in C and are delivered as executable programs (***.exe**). Since DokChess is developed in Java, they are of limited use as examples. Nothing is known in the project about chess communication protocols.

If it is not possible to make a working connection, the solution cannot be used with existing frontends. This not only lacks an important feature (refer V.1.1 Requirements Overview), but also makes the solution as a whole, especially as a case study, untrustworthy.

Eventuality Planning

A simple textual user interface could be implemented in order to interact with the engine. The implementation of a DokChess-specific graphical frontend would be costly (refer Risk V.11.2 Effort of Implementation).

Risk Minimization

Through an early proof of concept, certainty is achieved as soon as possible here.

11.2 Risk: Effort of Implementation

There is no experience with chess programming. Simultaneously, the rules that are to be implemented completely (see V1.1 *Requirements Overview*) are extensive and complicated. The different pieces move differently, and there are special rules such as stalemate and promotion. In the case of castling and en passant, the move history, and not only the current situation on the board, is relevant.

The programming of the algorithms is also non-trivial. For the connection of opening libraries and endgame databases, extensive research is required.

The implementation of DokChess runs as a hobby alongside, within the spare time. It is unclear whether this is sufficient to present ambitious results within schedule (refer V 2.2 *Constraints*).

Eventuality Planning

If there is no runnable version for the conference sessions in March and September 2011, a live demonstration could be omitted. The free evening talk at oose in March could even be canceled completely (which could negatively affect the reputation).

Risk Minimization

In order to reduce effort, the following rules are not implemented at first:

- 50 moves rule
- Threefold repetition

Their absence has little consequence with respect to the playing strength, and no consequence with respect to the correctness of the engine.

Connecting opening libraries and endgame databases has low priority and takes a back seat at first.

11.3 Risk: Reaching the Playing Strength

The quality goals demand both an acceptable playing strength and a simple, accessible solution. In addition, there are requirements with respect to efficiency. It is uncertain whether the planned Java solution with an object-oriented domain model and simple move selection can achieve these competing goals.

Eventuality Planning

In conference talks, parts of the live demonstration could be omitted. If necessary, we could show games played before.

Risk Minimization

Suitable scenarios (for example, see V.10 *Quality Scenarios*) concretize the quality goals. With the help of chess literature (chess problems to be precise) we develop test cases (unit testing) that specify what playing strength can be expected. Thus at least we detect early where the engine stands.

V.12 Glossary

"The game of chess is played between two opponents who move their pieces on a square board called a chessboard."

from the FIDE *Laws of Chess*

The following glossary contains English chess terms and terms from the world of computer chess. Some of them go beyond the vocabulary of infrequent or casual chess players.

See FIDE *Laws of Chess* or the *Wikipedia glossary of chess* for more information.

The names of the chess pieces are as shown in the following figure:

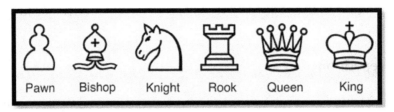

Figure 5.43: Chess pieces (or chessmen)

The chessboard geometry can be stated as follows:

"The chessboard is composed of an 8 x 8 grid of 64 equal squares alternately light (the 'white' squares) and dark (the 'black' squares)."

From the FIDE Laws of Chess

The following figure depicts the chessboard:

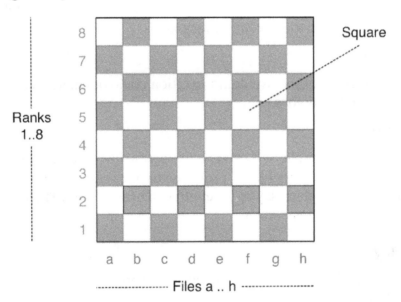

Figure 5.44: Chessboard

The following table describes the different terms in chess:

Term	Definition
50 move rule	A rule in chess, which states that a player can claim a *draw* after 50 moves whilst in the meantime no pawn has been moved and no piece has been taken.
Alpha-beta pruning	Significant improvement of the *Minimax algorithm*, in which parts of the search tree can be "cut off" without coming to a different resulting move.
Castling	A special move in chess where both the players's king and one the rooks are moved. For astling, different conditions must be met.
Chess 960	A chess variant developed by Bobby Fischer. The initial position is drawn from 960 ossibilities. Also known as Fischer Random Chess.
to drop (a piece)	A beginner's mistake in chess. A piece is dropped, if it is moved to a field attacked by the opponent and can be taken by him or her without risk or disadvantage.
Draw	A chess game which ends with no winner. There are various ways to end it with a draw, one of them is *stalemate*.
Half-move	Single action (move) of an individual player, unlike the sequence of a white and a black move which is counted as a move e.g. when numbering.
En passant	A special pawn move in chess. If a pawn moves on two squares and an opposing pawn could capture him, if he would advance only one square, the latter pawn may capture it en passant.
Endgame	The final stage of a chess game. It is characterised when only a few types of pieces are left on the board.
Engine	Part of a chess program which calculates the moves. Typically, an engine has no graphical user interface. Also known as 'chess engine'.
FEN	Forsyth-Edwards Notation. Compact representation of a chess board position as a character string. Supported by many chess tools. Used in DokChess by unit and integration tests. Explanation see e.g. Wikipedia (https://en.wikipedia.org/wiki/Forsyth–Edwards_Notation)
FIDE	Fédération Internationale des Échecs, international chess organisation
Fork	A tactic in chess in which a piece attacks two (or more) of the opponent's pieces simultaneously.
Knight fork	Particularly common form of a *fork* with a knight as attacking piece.
Mate	End of a chess game in which the king of the player to move is attacked and the player has no valid move left (i.e. can not escape the attack). The player has lost. Also known as 'checkmate'.
Minimax algorithm	Algorithm to determine the best move under the consideration of all options of both players.
Opening	First stage of a chess game. Knowledge and best practices of the first moves in chess fill many books and large databases.
Polyglot Opening Book	Binary file format for *opening* libraries. Unlike many other formats for this purpose the documentation of it is freely accessible.
Promotion	A rule in chess which states that a pawn who reached the opponent's base line is immediately converted into a queen, rook, bishop or knight.
Skewer	A tactic in chess in which a straight line passing piece stands on a rank, file or diagonal with two opponents pieces and forces the fore of the two pieces to move away.
Stalemate	End of a chess game in which the player to move does not have a valid move, but his or her king is not under attack. The game is considered a *draw*.
Threefold repetition	A rule in chess, which states that a player can claim a *draw* if the same position occurs at least three times.
WinBoard protocol	See *XBoard protocol*.
XBoard protocol	Text-based protocol for communication between chess frontends and *engines*. Also referred to as "WinBoard" or (more rarely) as "Chess Engine Communication Protocol".

Figure 5.45: Chess terms

6

VI - docToolchain

By **Ralf D. Müller**

docToolchain (https://doctoolchain.github.io/docToolchain/) initially began as the arc42-generator; that is, a Gradle build that converts the arc42 template from AsciiDoc to various other formats, such as Word, HTML, EPUB, and Confluence.

While working with AsciiDoc, I came up with several other little scripted tasks, which helped me in my workflow. These were added to the original arc42-generator and turned into what I now call "docToolchain."

The goal of docToolchain is to offer support to you, as a technical writer, with some repetitive conversion tasks, and also to enable you to implement the—sometimes quite complex—**Docs-as-Code** approach more easily.

I derived the name "docToolchain" from the fact that it implements a documentation toolchain. Several tools, such as Asciidoctor, Pandoc, and Microsoft Visio (to name a few), are glued together via Gradle to form a chain (or process) for all your documentation needs.

The following sections describe the architecture of docToolchain. The whole project, together with its remaining documentation, is hosted on GitHub at https://doctoolchain.github.io/docToolchain/.

VI.1 Introduction and Goals

The need to deliver an arc42 solution architecture in different formats was the primary driver that gave birth to docToolchain. As a technical person, I saw the value of text-based documentation. However, other stakeholders wanted to have the documentation:

- *"Where all other documentation is"*–in a wiki
- *"How we always document"*–with MS Word
- *"In a revision-safe format"*–as PDF

Soon, after fulfilling these needs, I noticed that it's quite hard to update changing UML diagrams. "Couldn't this be automated?," I thought to myself and created the *exportEA* task as a simple Visual Basic Script.

I didn't plan docToolchain on a drawing board. Instead, it evolved in an agile way; that is, through the requirements of the users.

Together with Dr. Gernot Starke, I gave a talk about this approach, and received some interesting feedback from the audience, such as *"... but I don't use Enterprise Architect–can I also use MS Visio?"*

My answer was something similar to the following:

"No, not at the moment. But docToolchain is not only a tool. I want it to be an idea–a change in how you think. If EA can be easily automated, I am sure Visio can be automated too!"

What I didn't expect was that, a few days after I made this statement, we got a pull request with the *exportVisio* task!

In this way, docToolchain evolved through the requirements and imagination of its users.

1.1 Problem Statement

The following figure depicts a problem to be solved by docToolchain:

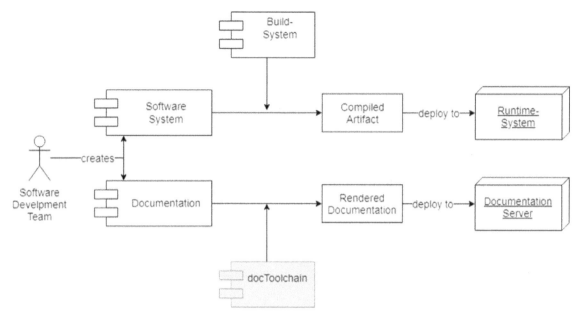

Figure 6.1: Problem statement mechanism

When a software development team creates a software system, a build system is used to create a compiled artifact, which is then deployed to the runtime system (refer to *Figure 6.1*).

You can apply the same approach to your documentation. This is called the *Docs-as-Code* approach; that is, you treat your documentation the same way as you treat your code. To do so, you need several helper scripts to automate repeating tasks to build your documentation; it is a waste of time setting up these tasks for each and every project from scratch.

docToolchain—the system described in this documentation—solves this problem by providing a set of build scripts that you can easily install. They provide you with a set of tasks to solve your standard Docs-as-Code needs.

The functional requirements are mainly split up into two different kinds of functionality:

- Tasks to export content from proprietary file formats to be used in AsciiDoc
- Tasks to generate or convert different output formats

These are then translated into architectural requirements:

RQ1: Build system integration

The system should be easy to integrate into a standard software build, in order to treat documents the same way as you treat your code.

RQ2: Easy to modify and extend

docToolchain should be easy to modify and extend.

There are many different functional requirements to a documentation toolchain—every user should be able to adapt it to their needs.

RQ3: Enterprise-ready

The project should run in different enterprise environments. It has to run with different version control systems and without direct access to the internet (only via proxies, for example, for dependency resolution).

Documentation is not only crucial for open source projects, but it is also essential for enterprise projects.

RQ4: Operating system-independent

The toolchain should run on Windows, Linux, and macOS.

This enables developers to use docToolchain on the operating system of their choice.

RQ5: Maven and Gradle

The toolchain should be available for the two major build systems, Maven and Gradle.

This ensures that most JVM-based projects can use it.

> **Note**
>
> RQ5 has been dropped for now (only Gradle is implemented)—please refer to DD3: Support for Maven and Gradle. A workaround through a mixed build is available.

RQ6: Clone, build, test, and run

The project should be set up in such a way that it runs right after you've cloned the repository.

This is to avoid the need for a special setup to be able to use it or for changing the project code.

1.2 Quality Goals

The main quality goals are the following:

- **QS1: Confidentiality**: This quality goal is not docToolchain-specific, but in terms of security, it is very important.

  Because the system is not only targeted for open source environments but for enterprise ones as well, we need to ensure that no data is sent to third-party systems without the user knowing it. For example, there are a number of server-based text analysis tools and libraries that send the text to be analyzed to a third-party server. Tools and libraries like these must not be used.

- **QS2: Ease of Use**: The docToolchain project is still a young open source project and, therefore, needs a stable and growing user base. The easiest way to achieve this is to make docToolchain extremely easy to use.

- **QS3: Maintainability**: There is no big company behind docToolchain—only users who evolve it in their spare time. Therefore, a developer should be able to make most changes needed to evolve docToolchain in a timebox of 1 to 3 hours.

1.3 Stakeholders

OSS Contributors: OSS Contributors (https://github.com/docToolchain/docToolchain/graphs/contributors) need to be aware of the architecture, in order to follow decisions and evolve the system in the right direction.

Contributors are mostly users of the system who need to fit a docToolchain task to their needs or need an additional task.

- **General docToolchain users**: These are mainly software architects and technical writers with a development background. It is very likely that a docToolchain user will also use arc42 and be familiar with it.

  The current focus is on users who are software architects in a corporate environment and work on the JVM with Git and Gradle.

  These users need to include architectural diagrams in their documentation and work in a restricted environment (such as with proxies, in local Maven repositories, with restricted internet access, and so on).

  They also need to be able to create different output formats for different stakeholders.

- **Users not working with the JVM**: docToolchain has also caught the attention of users who do not primarily work on the JVM. These users need to use docToolchain just like any other command-line tool.

- **Readers**: The main purpose of documentation is to be read by someone who needs specific information.

VI.2 Architecture Constraints

The following are the various architectural constraints:

- **C1: Run everywhere**: docToolchain has to run on all modern operating systems that users need for development, such as Windows, Linux, and macOS.

- **C2: Built for the JVM**: docToolchain is built for the JVM. While some of the features provided might also work together with other environments, this can't be guaranteed for all tasks.

- **C3: Enterprise-ready**: docToolchain has to run in restricted enterprise environments. It has to run with proxies, minimal dependencies, restricted internet access, and so on.

  This is also listed as requirement RQ3.

- **C4: Headless**: docToolchain has to run headless; that is, without a display, to run on build servers. User interaction and Windows features have to be avoided.

VI.3 System Scope and Context

This chapter describes the various contexts for which docToolchain is designed, including its functional scope.

Business Context

The following diagram shows the business context in which docToolchain operates:

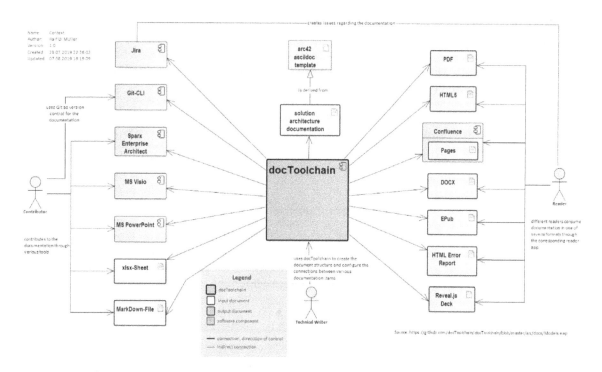

Figure 6.2: Business context

The preceding diagram is correct regarding the connections from docToolchain; however, the relationships between the two actors, **Contributor** and **Reader**, are abstract.

These actors represent users who contribute to the documentation or access it. The connections shown between the actors and the neighbor systems are abstract because these users do not directly access the files. In addition to this, they might use different applications to read and modify the content.

docToolchain itself uses exactly the applications shown or reads and modifies files directly.

It creates output documents directly as file content. Note that, only for Confluence, the Confluence API and, therefore, **Confluence as a System** is used.

To read the input documents, docToolchain often needs an application that can be remote-controlled to convert and read them. However, it does directly read XLSX and Markdown files.

The actors represent roles. Each user can access the system through all of those roles. Each user will likely have a primary role.

The **Reader** and **Contributor** roles don't have a direct connection to docToolchain. They may read and modify content through different applications than docToolchain uses in order to access the content. Following table depicts the important entities in the docToolchain.

Actor / Neighbor	Description
Technical Writer (user)	These are the users who use docToolchain to manage their documentation. They create the document structure and configure the connection between different documentation items mainly via include[111]- and image[112]-directives in AsciiDoc.
Contributor (user)	These are the users who contribute to the documentation of the Technical Writer not necessarily knowing of docToolchain. They may use different applications to modify the content.
Reader (user)	These are the users who consume the documentation created by the Technical Writer and additional contributors. They use several reader applications for this task.
Jira (external system)	Issue tracking system from which docToolchain may export issues to be included in the documentation
Git-Repository (external system)	Version control system from which docToolchain may export change log information to be included in the documentation
Sparx Enterprise Architect (external system)	UML modeling tool from which docToolchain may export diagrams (as images) and element notes to be included in the documentation
MS Visio (external system)	Diagramming tool from which docToolchain may export diagrams (as images) and notes to be included in the documentation
MS PowerPoint (external system)	Presentation tool from which docToolchain may export slides (as images) and speaker notes to be included in the documentation
xlsx-sheet (input document)	Spreadsheet document which may be transformed into AsciiDoc by docToolchain to be included in the documentation
MarkDown-File (input document)	Document which may be transformed into AsciiDoc by docToolchain to be included in the documentation
your solution architecture documentation (AsciiDoc-document)	The main document which references all other parts of your documentation through include-statements. For a solution architecture, this document is derived from the arc42-template
arc42 template (as AsciiDoc-document)	The template that helps you to structure the documentation of your solution architecture
docToolchain (system)	the system that is described here
PDF (output file)	One of several output formats in which docToolchain can render documentation
HTML5 (output file)	One of several output formats in which docToolchain can render documentation
Confluence (external system)	The well known Wiki to which docToolchain can publish documentation
DOCX (output file)	One of several output formats in which docToolchain can render documentation
EPub (output file)	One of several output formats in which docToolchain can render documentation
HTML Error Report (output file)	To check the quality of the documentation, docToolchain can create an error report which contains the results of some syntax check on the generated HTML documents
Reveal.js Deck (output file)	One of several output formats in which docToolchain can render documentation

Figure 6.3: Actors of docToolchain

Technical Context

This section describes the technical interfaces of the components listed in the preceding table:

System	Interface
Jira (external system)	REST-API
Git-Repository (external system)	Shell execution of commands
Sparx Enterprise Architect (external system)	COM-API through execution of a Visual Basic Script
MS Visio (external system)	"COM-API through execution of a Visual Basic Script"
MS PowerPoint (external system)	"COM-API through execution of a Visual Basic Script"
xlsx-sheet (input document)	Apache POI Java library
MarkDown-File (input document)	"nl.jworks.markdown_to_asciidoc Java library"
PDF (output file)	Asciidoctor PDF Plugin
HTML5 (output file)	Asciidoctor
Confluence (external system)	REST-API
DOCX (output file)	"conversion of docBook file (generated by Asciidoctor) via pandoc"
EPub (output file)	"conversion of docBook file (generated by Asciidoctor) via pandoc"
HTML Error Report (output file)	via htmlSanityCheck
Reveal.js Deck (output file)	additional Asciidoctor backend

Figure 6.4: Description of technical interfaces

Scope

This section explains the scope of docToolchain; for example, what types of tasks docToolchain is responsible for, as well as what it is not responsible for.

docToolchain can be described as the following:

- It is a collection of tasks used to make creating and maintaining documentation easier.
- It tries to delegate tasks to other available tools wherever possible.

docToolchain does *not* do the following:

- Reimplement tasks of other available tools
- Modify manually created content
- Serve the generated content and is not a build server for documents

VI.4 Solution Strategy

This chapter describes the strategy we used to approach problems in the past and how we will approach them in the future.

General Solution Strategy

The first docToolchain tasks evolved from standalone scripts that were executed from the command line. The next logical step was to include them in a build system.

In Gradle, it is relatively straightforward to be able to include a Groovy-based script as a new task:

```
task newTask (
    description: 'just a demo',
    group: 'docToolchain'
)  {
    doLast {
        // here you can put any Groovy script
    }
}
```

The original **build.gradle** soon grew into a huge single file. To make it more modular, we split it up into so-called **script-plugins** (https://docs.gradle.org/current/userguide/plugins.html#sec:script_plugins). You extract tasks that belong together in an extra **.gradle** file (for docToolchain, you will find these in the **/scripts** folder) and reference them from the main **build.gradle**:

```
apply from: 'script/exportEA.gradle'
```

To make docToolchain easier to use, one recommendation is to move those script plugins to binary plugins. These plugins reference a precompiled **.jar** file from a repository instead of downloaded scripts.

Individual Solution Strategy

The solution strategy for individual tasks can be broken up into two main classes of tasks.

Export Tasks

These are tasks that export diagrams and plain text from other tools. All tools are different, so most of them need individual solution strategies.

These tools often save their data in a proprietary binary data format, which is not easy to put under version control.

The solution strategy for exporting tasks is to first try and read the file format directly to export the data. An excellent example of this is the *exportExcel* task, which uses the Apache POI library (https://poi.apache.org/) to access the file directly. This solution makes the task independent of MS Excel itself.

However, there are tools for which the file format can't be read directly, or the effort is too great. In those cases, the solution strategy is to automate the tool itself. An excellent example of this is the *exportEA* task, where the task starts **Enterprise Architect** (**EA**) in an invisible, headless mode and exports all diagrams and notes through the COM interface. The drawbacks are that this task only runs on Windows systems. It can also be slow and, while Enterprise Architect is invisible, it still claims the input focus so you can't work with the machine during export. However, besides those drawbacks, the automation is still valuable.

The third kind of tool that docToolchain can export data from includes web-based tools such as Atlassian Jira. Here, the obvious solution is to use the available REST API to export it. There is also a Java API that wraps the REST API; however, the direct REST API is preferred.

Version Control of Exported Artifacts

Most export tasks are quite slow; that is, so slow that you don't want to run them every time you generate your documentation. In addition to this, some of the exports (such as *exportEA*) don't run on a Linux-based build server. Because of this, the general strategy is to put the exported artifacts under version control. The tasks create *special* folders into which they place—among the exported data—a **README.adoc** file that warns the user that the files in the folder will be overwritten with the next export.

It might sound strange, at first, to put exported or generated artifacts under version control, but you do get an additional benefit. The exported files—in contrast to their proprietary source files—can be easily compared and reviewed!

When a software system has a longer lifetime, it might be that some of the input systems get outdated. This may result in unreadable source files. In these cases, the version-controlled artifacts might also be quite useful since they are in easy-to-read, text-only, or image formats.

Generate Tasks

These are tasks that generate different output formats from the sources.

For these tasks, the general solution strategy should be to implement them as an additional Asciidoctor backend (as **reveal.js** does, for example), or at least as a plugin (as the PDF plugin does, for example). However, the effort required to create an Asciidoctor backend is, due to missing documentation, quite substantial.

So, we use two other solution approaches:

- Conversion from another already available format (**HTML >> Confluence**)
- Conversion via Pandoc (Docx, EPUB)

VI.5 Building Block View

The following are the different levels for building blocks:

5.1 Level 1

The following diagram shows the building blocks of level 1:

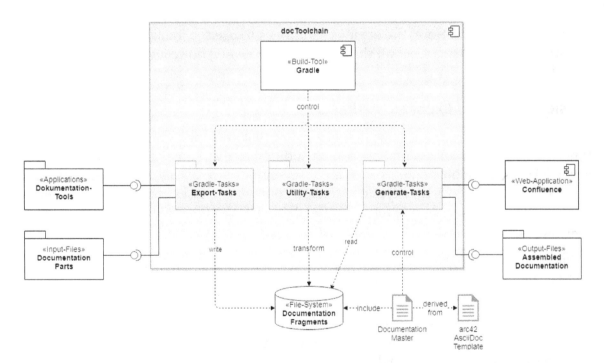

Figure 6.5 Level 1 building block

The following table describes the different components of the building block level 1:

Component	Description
Gradle	This is the Gradle build system which is used for docToolchain to orchestrate the documentation tasks. Details can be found at https://gradle.org
Documentation Tools	These are various tools which are used to create parts of your system documentation. Popular examples are MS Word and MS PowerPoint. docToolchain interfaces these tools directly instead reading the source files because there is no known direct file API for these tools. *See level 2: Documentation Tools* for details.
Documentation Source Files	Some parts of your documentation might be created in a format for which a direct file API exists. This package contains those input files.
Export Tasks	This package contains several tasks which export data from Documentation Tools by either interfacing the Documentation Tools or accessing the Documentation Source Files directly. *See level 2: Export Tasks* for details.
Documentation Fragments	All parts of your documentation which where exported from another source are stored in the file system for further processing.
Utility Tasks	This is a collection of Gradle tasks which do not belong to the export- or generate-tasks. *See level 2: Utility Tasks* for details.
Generate Tasks	All generate tasks have in common that they use the *documentation master* to generate the assembled documentation in a specific output format. This package contains all of these tasks. *See level 2: Generate Tasks* for details.
Confluence	Confluence is the well-known enterprise wiki created by Atlassian. Details can be found at https://www.atlassian.com/confluence.
Assembled Documentation	The goal of docToolchain is to assemble system architecture documentation. This package is the target for the various output files.
Documentation Master	This is the heart of your documentation. It uses AsciiDoc as markup language to implement your documentation. The include-directive of AsciiDoc is used to reference all Documentation Fragments at the correct location of your documentation. Through this mechanism, it controls how the documentation is assembled from the various input sources. There can be more than one documentation master, for instance one for each type of documentation and each stakeholder.
arc42 AsciiDoc Template	Since docToolchain is about system architecture documentation, the best way to get started is to derive the Documentation Master from the arc42 AsciiDoc Template. The template can be found at https://arc42.org/download

Figure 6.6: Description of building block level 1 components

5.2 Level 2

The following are the different types of tasks included in level 2 of building blocks.

5.2.1 Export Tasks

The following figure depicts the export task block of level 2 building blocks:

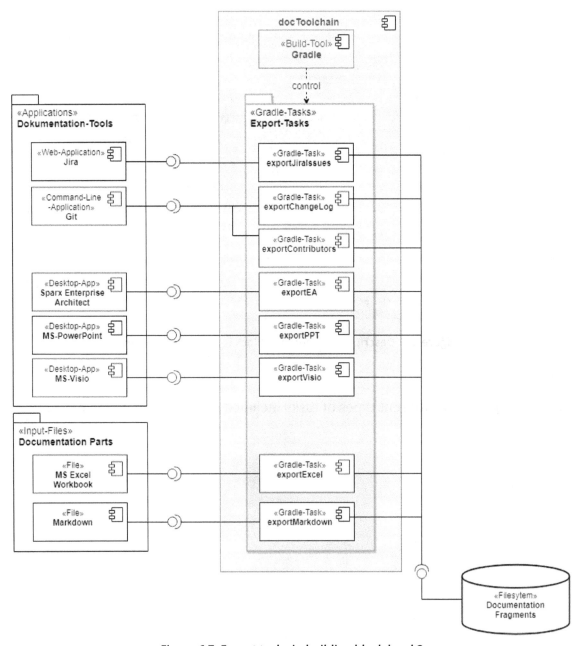

Figure 6.7: Export tasks in building block level 2

Documentation Tools and Export Tasks

These are the tools that docToolchain is able to export documentation fragments from. Each tool is interfaced with at least one export task through a specific interface:

Component	Description
Jira & exportJiraIssues	Jira is the issue tracking system from Atlassian. The *exportJiraIssues* task exports a list of issues for a given JQL-Search. These issues are exported through the Jira Server REST API. The result is stored as an AsciiDoc table to be included from the *Documentation Master*. More documentation for this task can be found in the manual.
Git, exportChangeLog & exportContributors	Git is directly invoked as command-line tool trough Groovy. The *exportChangeLog* task exports the list of change messages from git for the documentation folder as an AsciiDoc table to be included from the *Documentation Master*. More documentation for this task can be found in the manual. The exportContributors task exports the list of contributors and additional file attributes from git for all AsciiDoc files. This information is stored as AsciiDoc files to be included from the *Documentation Master*. More documentation for this task can be found in the manual.
Sparx EA & exportEA	Sparx Enterprise Architect (EA) is the UML modeling tool from Sparx Systems. The *exportEA* task exports all diagrams and element notes from a model through the COM API provided by EA. The API is interfaced through a Visual Basic Script started from the task. The COM API is more an application remoting interface than a data access interface. As a result, docToolchain starts EA headless and iterates through the model in order to export the data. The resulting images and text files can be included from the *Documentation Master*. More documentation for this task can be found in the manual.
MS-PowerPoint & exportPPT	MS-PowerPoint is the presentation software from Microsoft. The *exportPPT* task exports all Slides of a slide-deck as .png image files together with the speaker notes as text files. As interface, the COM API provided by PowerPoint is used through a Visual Basic Script which is started from the task. MS-PowerPoint is used in this case because it has a quite usable API. But the slide decks can also be created and modified with other presentation tools. The resulting images and text files can be included from the Documentation Master. More documentation for this task can be found in the manual.
MS-Visio & exportVisio	MS-Visio is the diagramming software from Microsoft. The *exportVisio* task exports all diagrams as image files together with their corresponding diagram notes as text files. As interface, the COM API provided by Visio is used through a Visual Basic Script which is started from the task. The resulting images and text files can be included from the Documentation Master. *More documentation* for this task can be found in the manual.
Documentation Parts & Export Tasks	These are files which can be directly interfaced by docToolchain without the need of an additional tool. Each file is interfaced by one export task through a certain library.
MS-Excel Workbook & exportExcel	MS-Excel is the spreadsheet software from Microsoft. The *exportExcel* task exports all spreadsheets contained in a .xlsx-workbook as CSV-files and AsciiDoc-Tables to be included from the *Documentation Master*. As interface, the Apache POI library is used. More documentation for this task can be found in the manual.
MarkDown & exportMarkdown	MarkDown is the well-known, and quite popular markup language. The *exportMarkdown* task exports all .md files found in the documentation folder to AsciiDoc to be included from the *Documentation Master*. The interface is a direct file access and as converter the nl.jworks.markdown_to_asciidoc library is used. More documentation for this task can be found in the manual.

Figure 6.8: Description of export tasks components

Utility Tasks

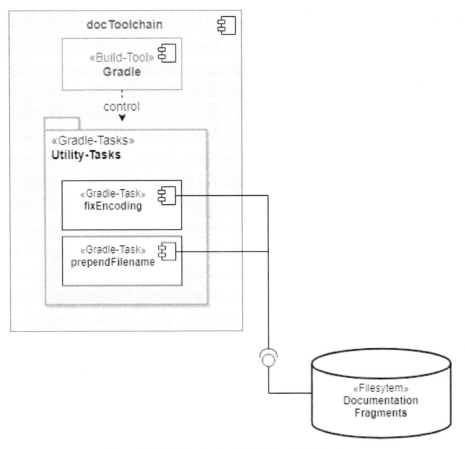

Figure 6.9: Utility tasks in building blocks view

These are tasks that might be helpful in certain situations but do not directly belong to the scope of docToolchain:

Component	Description
fixEncoding	Asciidoctor is very strict regarding the encoding. It needs UTF-8 as file encoding. But sometimes a text editor or some operation on your documentation file might change the encoding. In this case, this task will help. It reads all documentation files with the given or guessed encoding and rewrites them in UTF-8. More documentation for this task can be found in the manual.
prependFilename	This task is a workaround for the behavior of the Asciidoctor include-directive: in Asciidoctor, there is no way to determine the name of the currently rendered file, only of the master document. But for features like the list of contributors or a link back to the git sources, the name of the currently rendered file is needed. This task crawls trough all AsciiDoc files and prepends their filename to solve this problem. More documentation for this task can be found in the manual.

Figure 6.10: Description of utility components

5.2.4 Generate Tasks

The following figure depicts the Generate-Tasks block in level 2 building blocks:

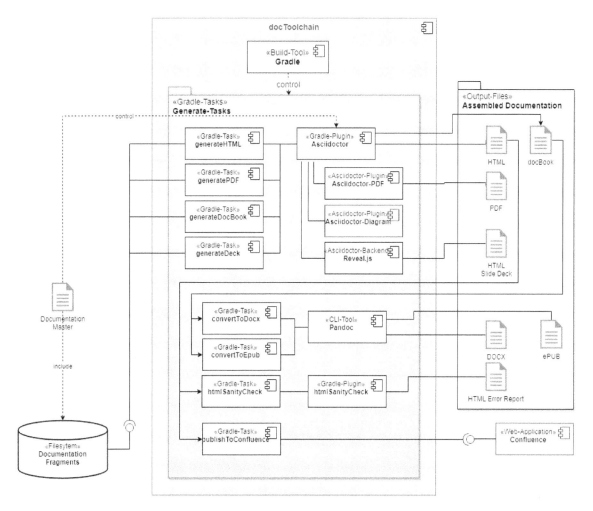

Figure 6.11: Generating tasks

This package contains all the tasks that assemble your documentation to various output files in different formats:

Component	Description
Asciidoctor	Asciidoctor as rendering engine is at the heart of this package. docToolchain uses Asciidoctor as Gradle plugin which wraps the Ruby implementation with jRuby. This is mostly transparent for the user, but it is important in the enterprise context: all Asciidoctor plugins also refer to their wrapped versions and not the Ruby gems. This way, we avoid to reference the Ruby gem repository as an external dependency for docToolchain. Instead, all wrapped plugins are referenced from the standard Java repositories. More details can be found at https://asciidoctor.org/docs/asciidoctorgradle-plugin/
Asciidoctor-PDF	Asciidoctor needs this plugin to render your document as PDF. More details can be found at https://asciidoctor.org/docs/asciidoctor-pdf/
Asciidoctor-Diagram	This plugin enables several text-based diagram formats like plantUML. They can be specified inline as textual representation. See https://asciidoctor.org/docs/asciidoctordiagram/ and http://plantuml.com/ for more details.
Reveal.js	Asciidoctor parses the input file and renders each parsed element through defined markup fragments. A collection of those fragments is called a rendering backend. The Reveal.js backend is capable of rendering AsciiDoc as HTML which is turned into a slide presentation through some clever styles and JavaScript. See https://asciidoctor.org/docs/asciidoctorrevealjs/ for more details.
generateHTML	This is the most straightforward task which generates the standard HTML output with the help of the Asciidoctor Gradle Plugin. Takes as input the Master Documentation which includes the Documentation Fragments. More documentation for this task can be found in the manual.
generatePDF	This task is equal to the generateHTML task, but it uses the Asciidoctor-PDF Asciidoctor Plugin to generate a PDF file as output. Takes as input the Master Documentation which includes the Documentation Fragments. More documentation for this task can be found in the manual.
generateDocBook	This task is equal to the generateHTML task but produces a docBook XML-file as output. It uses the Asciidoctor Gradle Plugin for this task. Takes as input the Master Documentation which includes the Documentation Fragments. More documentation for this task can be found in the manual.
generateDeck	This task uses the Reveal.js Asciidoctor backend to generate an HTML based slide deck. Takes as input the Master Documentation which includes the Documentation Fragments. More documentation for this task can be found in the manual.
convertToDocx & convertToEpub	These two tasks use Pandoc as command-line tool to convert the generated HTML documentation into a DOCx or ePub file. More documentation for this task can be found in the manual.
htmlSanityCheck	This task runs a check on the generated HTML documentation. It uses the Gradle Plugin of the same name to perform this task. It generates a Unit-Test like HTML Error Report. See https://github.com/aim42/htmlSanityCheck for more details.
publishToConfluence	This task takes the generated HTML output and splits it by the headline levels into separate pages. These pages and their images are then published to a Confluence instance. It uses the confluence REST API to interface Confluence. More documentation for this task can be found in the manual.
Confluence	Confluence is the well-known enterprise wiki created by Atlassian. Details can be found at https://www.atlassian.com/confluence .
Pandoc	Pandoc is "the swiss army knife for markup conversion". It is used to generate DOCx and ePub files. See https://pandoc.org/ for more details.

Figure 6.12: Description of components in generating tasks

VI.6 Runtime View

There are no special runtime situations that need to be explained as a sequence diagram. However, the following diagrams shows the flow of information through the toolchain:

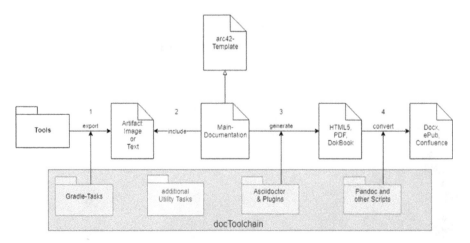

Figure 6.13: Runtime view: abstract flow

The preceding figure can be explained as follows:

1. docToolchain exports data (that is, diagram images and plain text) from documentation tools.

2. The main documentation (on the basis of the arc42 template) includes the exported artifacts.

3. The final output is generated via Asciidoctor and plugins.

4. It is finally converted through additional scripts and tools.

Besides this, docToolchain contains some additional utility tasks that do not directly fit into the preceding schema, such as the *HtmlSanityCheck* task.

The following diagram shows the details of all the currently implemented tasks. It focuses on the various input artifacts, which are transformed through the Gradle tasks that make up docToolchain. Each connection is either a Gradle task that transforms the artifact or an AsciiDoc **include** directive that references the input artifacts from the main documentation, and thus instructs Asciidoctor to assemble the whole documentation:

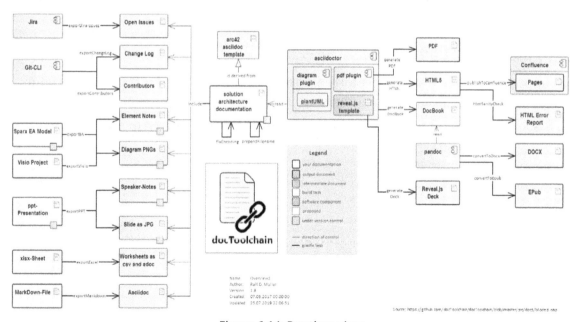

Figure 6.14: Runtime view

VI.7 Deployment View

docToolchain is only used to generate documentation and is, therefore, not deployed to a production environment. However, depending on your requirements, you might want to deploy it not only to your development machine but also to a build server.

The general deployment is done by cloning the docToolchain source repository. Depending on your needs, the details will vary.

7.1 Option 1: Installed the Command-Line Tool

For this option, you clone the docToolchain repository to a location outside of the project you want to write the documentation for. You then add the **<docToolchain home>/bin** folder to your **PATH** variable. Now you can use docToolchain as a command-line tool:

```
doctoolchain <docDir> <task>
```

This approach works quite well and is independent of your project. However, it violates RQ6 (clone, build, test, and run) for your project. Someone who clones your project will also have to install docToolchain before they can work on the documentation. Also, making any changes in docToolchain is likely to break your build if you do not update docToolchain on all systems.

7.2 Option 2: Git Submodule

This approach is the currently preferred option. Here, you add docToolchain to your project by adding it as a Git submodule:

```
git submodule add https://github.com/docToolchain/docToolchain.git
```

This preceding line of code adds one additional folder to your project, containing the whole docToolchain repository:

```
yourProject/
├─ docToolchain/    <--    docToolchain as submodule
├─ src/
│      ├─ docs      <--    docs for yourProject
│      ├─ test      <--    tests for yourProject
│      └─ java      <--    sources of yourProject
├─ ...
├─ build.gradle     <--    build of yourProject
├─ ...
```

As you can see, this provides a clean separation between your project and docToolchain. The `git submodule` is just a pointer to the docToolchain repository–not a copy. It points to a specific release. This approach ensures that whoever clones your project also gets the correct version of docToolchain.

To use docToolchain with this approach, you configure it as a subproject of your main Gradle project (you can find further details in this tutorial at https://docs-as-co.de/getstarted/tutorial2).

If your project uses another build system, such as Maven, you can still use this approach. You simply use Maven to build your code and Gradle to build your documentation.

See also: TR3: Git Submodules

7.3 Option 3: Docker Container

Last but not least, you can deploy docToolchain as a command-line tool to a Docker container. This can then be used in various ways (for instance, in a GitLab pipeline).

VI.8 Cross cutting Concepts

Because of the nature of docToolchain (as a locally used development tool), most of the standard cross cutting concepts (for example, security, monitoring, and so on) do not apply.

This is why this section is short.

Automated Testing

In an ideal world, we would have covered all code with unit tests. However, currently, the smallest unit of docToolchain is a Gradle task. Because of the dependencies on Gradle, we can't easily test these tasks in isolation.

The current solution for automated tests is to use the **gradleTestKit** (https://docs.gradle.org/4.9/userguide/userguide.html) and **Spock** (http://spockframework.org/).

Through the gradleTestKit, Gradle will start another Gradle instance with its own test configurations. The gradleTestKit ensures that all tasks can be integration-tested in an automated way.

Spock helps to define the tests in an easy-to-maintain, **behavior-driven development** (**BDD**, https://en.wikipedia.org/wiki/Behavior-driven_development) way.

VI.9 Design Decisions

This section lists the important design decisions that were made while docToolchain has evolved. They fulfill two tasks:

- Explain to users and contributors who are new to the project why things are the way that they are

- Help to revise decisions for which the base has changed

DD1: Wrapped Plugins instead of Ruby Gems

Problem: Asciidoctor plugins can be referenced directly as Ruby gems or as Java dependencies to the JRuby-wrapped .jar files. While Ruby gems always provide the latest version, it might take a number of days for the JRuby versions to become available. Both types of plugins are downloaded from different repositories. In an enterprise environment, the Ruby Gems repository might not be accessible. Since the user of docToolchain is likely to be a JVM developer, and Gradle already depends on Java repositories, the Ruby Gems repository is an additional dependency and would violate C3: *Enterprise-ready*.

Decision: docToolchain will always use the JRuby version because the necessary `.jar` files can be downloaded from the same repository as all the other Java dependencies.

Decided by *Ralf D. Müller*, April 2017 (https://rdmueller.github.io/enterprise-edition2/)

DD2: Visual Basic Script for EA Automation

Problem: The UML-tool *Enterprise Architect* by Sparx Systems can be interfaced in several ways.

Via internal scripts

This requires a change in the setup of the project's EA project.

Via the Sparx Java API or a COM Bridge such as JaCoB

Both solutions require a *DLL* to be installed. This violates C3: *Enterprise-ready*. In addition to this, our experience has shown that the Java API (at the time it was tested) wasn't free of flaws.

Via Visual Basic

This requires some Visual Basic know-how instead of the already available Java experience.

Decision: The first approach isn't easy, and the second even violates a constraint. So, it was decided that Visual Basic would be used as an automation tool. Since this is the native interface for a COM object (which Enterprise Architect provides), the amount of bugs in the interface is expected to be minimal. For a first POC, I used Visual Basic together with Visual Studio. This setup provides IntelliSense and code completion features, and thus makes it easy to explore the API. However, the final task uses Visual Basic Script, which is a little bit different and doesn't provide you with code completion features.

Decided by *Ralf D. Müller*, August 2016.

DD3: Support for Maven and Gradle

Problem: I initially planned to support the two major build systems known to me: Maven and Gradle. While Asciidoctor supports both build systems through plugins, I soon noticed that even basic features such as PlantUML and PDF generation are hard to maintain for both systems. In addition to this, some features are easy (for me) to implement through Gradle and harder to implement in Maven.

Decision: Support for Maven has been dropped.

Decided by *Ralf D. Müller*, August 2016

DD4: Binary Gradle Plugins

Problem: docToolchain consists of Gradle script plugins. Some developers don't consider these plugins a clean approach and think that they make it harder to use docToolchain (see *Deployment View*).

However, script plugins also have advantages. They make the code more compact and easier to maintain because they consist of single files and are not distributed over several classes. The tasks are often so small that we included their source in the manual of docToolchain. When a user reads through the manual, they see at once how the tasks are implemented. The chances are that such a user will turn into a contributor after acquiring this knowledge.

Decision: The pros of using script plugins currently weigh more than the cons. docToolchain has to be easy to maintain and extendable (see RQ2: *Easy to modify and extend*).

There is one exception to this rule: some tasks—such as the Pandoc task—are just wrappers to other executables. A binary plugin could even help in this situation by providing an automated download of the executable. (In fact, the first version of a binary Pandoc plugin is already available at https://github.com/docToolchain/pandocGradlePlugin.)

Decided by Ralf D. Müller, mid. 2018

DD5: AsciiDoc as Basis

Problem: In order to follow the Docs-as-Code approach, a format for writing documentation is needed that is solely based on plain text. Binary formats—mainly used by word processors—are not very well suited for the tools used by a developer and, therefore, are not suited for the Docs-as-Code approach.

There are several plain text markup formats available, such as Markdown, Restructured Text, Latex, and AsciiDoc.

Decision: docToolchain uses AsciiDoc as a markup format to write documentation. AsciiDoc is easy to use but it is also powerful, and it has already proved that it is perfect for writing technical documentation.

DD6: Deployment Options

Problem: docToolchain is not an application that can be deployed to a server. So, there is no standard pattern for the deployment of docToolchain.

Decision: The most common options to use (that is, deploy) docToolchain are the three described in *Deployment View*.

Considered alternatives: The following deployment options have been considered but not implemented.

DD6.1: Embedded

This was the first approach used but we do not recommend it anymore. In this approach, you use docToolchain itself as a base project, and add all the code and documentation to that base project.

This approach makes it hard to update docToolchain itself, since docToolchain and your project are mangled together:

```
yourProject/
├── scripts/                <-- docToolchain task definitions
│   ├── AsciiDocBasics.gradle
│   │   ...
│   └── publishToConfluence.gradle
├── docs/                   <-- docToolchain rendered manual
├── resources/              <-- docToolchain external submodules
├── src/
│   ├── docs                <-- docs for docToolchain AND yourProject
│   ├── test                <-- tests for docToolchain AND yourProject
│   └── java                <-- sources of yourProject
├── ...
├──  build.gradle <-- merged build file of docToolchain
├── ...   AND yourProject
```

As you can see, this was only a good idea in the beginning, when docToolchain mainly consisted of an extended Asciidoctor build template.

DD6.2: Gradle Script Plugins

This approach is currently a theoretical option. It has not been used yet but is mentioned here for the sake of completeness.

Gradle has a feature called script plugins. In the same way that docToolchain references the modular, local Gradle files for different tasks:

```
apply from: 'scripts/exportExcel.gradle'
```

You can also reference these scripts as remote files in your project's **build.gradle** file:

```
apply from: 'https://github.com/docToolchain/docToolchain/blob/b415bfb/\

scripts/exportExcel.gradle'
```

This line references an exact version of the file – so, as long as you trust GitHub and your connection to GitHub, this approach is safe and works for all self-contained tasks.

DD6.3: Gradle Binary Plugins

You can refer to DD4: *Binary Gradle Plugins* to find out why this was not an option in the past.

For this option, the existing script plugins have to be converted binary plugins for Gradle.

As a result, they can be referenced directly from your **build.gradle** file. HTML Sanity Check is an excellent example of this approach:

```
plugins {
    id "org.aim42.htmlSanityCheck" version "1.0.0-RC-2"
}
```

We could turn docToolchain into a binary plugin that references all other plugins as its dependency. Alternatively, we could turn docToolchain into a collection of binary plugins, and a user of docToolchain would reference those plugins they require.

VI.10 Quality Requirements

QS1: Confidentiality

In order to keep control over the content of your documentation, docToolchain will never use a web-based, remote service for any task without the explicit knowledge of the user.

QS2: Security (besides Confidentiality)

When you think of documentation, security is not the first thing that comes to mind, is it?

However, when you automate some parts of your documentation, or even just include remote sources, security comes into play.

It could even be that you use a plugin (such as the asciidoctorj-screenshot plugin, which is available at https://github.com/asciidoctor/asciidoctorj-screenshot) that lets you execute arbitrary code in the generation phase.

In docToolchain, we assume that the documentation is under your control, and hence, do not apply any special security measures besides respecting QS1: *Confidentiality*.

QS3: Repeatability

Every run of a docToolchain task creates the same predictable output.

This rule ensures that it doesn't matter if you move the source or the generated output from stage to stage.

QS4: Transformation Stability

No docToolchain task will remove content. Tasks (such as the export task) may only add content. This rule is to ensure that all generated content contains the same information.

However, some formats might not be able to display the same layout and text style.

QS5: Performance

Functionality first; docToolchain is about the automation of repetitive manual tasks. So, even when an automated task is slow, it will have value.

However, we should strive for better performance whenever we see a chance to optimize tasks.

QS6: Ease of Use

docToolchain should be as easy to use as possible. The goal is that docToolchain is easy to install and that the use of all tasks does not require any additional knowledge about the inner workings of the system.

Currently, a single binary Gradle plugin is seen as the right solution to achieve this quality goal, but it is not on the roadmap yet (you can also refer to DD4: Binary Gradle Plugins).

QS7: Maintainability

Many users with different needs use docToolchain. Those different needs are the result of the different environments and different tools that are in use.

Therefore, docToolchain tasks should be easy to modify to fit everyone's needs; that is, at least those tasks that are not stable yet.

There should also be blueprints for new tasks.

The "easy to modify" quality goal is currently achieved through the scripting character of the Gradle script plugins. The source is referenced from the documentation and is easy to understand—therefore, it is easy to modify.

However, this is in contrast to the "Ease of Use" quality goal; that is, script plugins versus binary plugins.

VI.11 Risks and Technical Debts

This section describes the risks that might be posed by using docToolchain and how they are—from an architectural point of view—mitigated.

TR1: Outdated Technology

Description: A software system might live for several decades. During that time, some parts of the toolchain might get outdated. For instance, a UML modeler you didn't buy a new license for.

In such cases, you might not be able to regenerate parts of your documentation.

Mitigation: The biggest risk of this kind is related to the proprietary tools the diagrams and texts are exported from. docToolchain exports these artifacts, not to the **/build** folder, but to the **/src/docs** folder on purpose:

- If one of the tools gets outdated, you still have the exported data, and therefore, you can still work with it.

- In addition, exported **.png** images and plain text files are easier to compare than binary source formats, which come often. This enables you to better review the changes in your documentation.

TR2: Missing Acceptance of the Docs-as-Code Approach

Description: When you start to use docToolchain and thus implement the Docs-as-Code approach, there's a risk that colleagues may not accept this "new" approach.

In our experience, this is a low risk. We've never seen someone switch back to MS Word from AsciiDoc. However, it might give users a good feeling to be able to do so.

Mitigation: You can convert your documents to several output formats, such as PDF, MS Word, and Confluence. This not only gives you a fallback when you reach a point where you think that the Docs-as-Code approach doesn't fit your requirements, but it also allows you to work together with colleagues who haven't transitioned to Docs-as-Code yet.

TR3: Git Submodules

Description: Git submodules are great in theory. As soon as you use them, you will notice that it requires a bit of practice:

- If added via an SSH protocol, users without SSH configured for their Git account won't be able to clone them.

- Submodules can easily get into a *detached head* state.

- At least Git on Windows has authentication problems with submodules (the use of Pageant helps).

This could lower the acceptance of docToolchain in general.

Mitigation:

- Always use HTTP to add a submodule.

- Someone should write a *Guide to Git Submodules* for docToolchain.

TR4: Automated Tests (Technical Debt)

Description: The project does not have good test coverage. This is because the Travis checks often break.

Mitigation: There is no appropriate mitigation yet, besides working on the test coverage.

VI.12 Glossary

Term	Definition
COM, Component Object Model	COM is an interface technology defined and implemented as a standard by Microsoft. See also COM on Wikipedia
COM-Bridge	A library which allows you to use one technology from within another. In this case, it allows you to access the COM-interface from within Java programs.
DLL, Dynamic-Link Library	Dynamic-link library (or DLL) is Microsoft's implementation of the shared library concept in the Microsoft Windows and OS/2 operating systems. See also DLL on Wikipedia
EA, Enterprise Architect	A UML modeling tool by Sparx Systems. See EA on Wikipedia
JACOB	A Java-COM-Bridge. See https://sourceforge.net/projects/jacobproject/ fordetails
POC, Proof of Concept	Minimalistic code that proofs a certain idea
Sparx, Sparx Systems	The company behind Enterprise Architect
Task	Tasks are the smallest entity of the toolchain. A docToolchain task is implemented as Gradle task.

Figure 6.15: Glossary terms

VII - macOS Menu Bar Application

By **Dr. Gernot Starke**

This surely is one of the shortest and most compact architecture documentations.

Its goal is to show that arc42 can be tailored to suit your needs and be reduced to keep only a minimal amount of documentation.

I implemented this example as a brief excursion into the Swift programming language. I did not want to invest too much time on the documentation, although I wanted to highlight the most important facts about this implementation.

The result: a few keywords on requirements, the names of some important OS classes, and a few links to resources that I found useful during implementation.

I used a mindmap instead of text, tables, and diagrams:

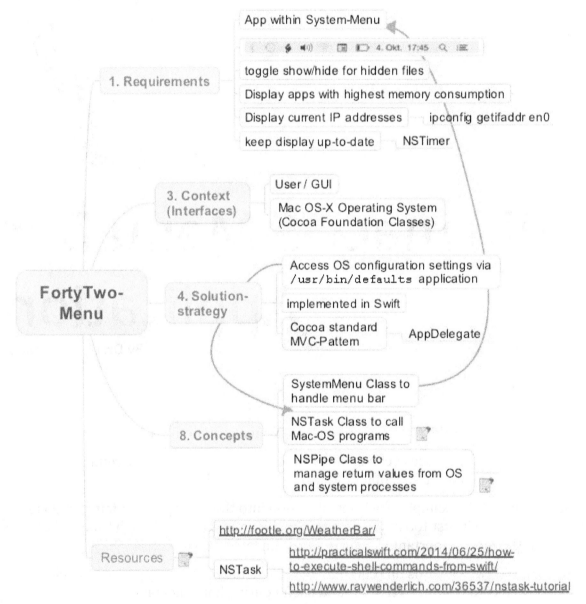

Figure 7.1: Extremely short documentation

Index

About

All major keywords used in this book are captured alphabetically in this section. Each one is accompanied by the page number of where they appear.